MOVING TO MÉRIDA

How To Successfully Move To Mexico As A Family

CASSIE PEARSE

❀ Created with Vellum

Contents

Introduction   vii

1. How Did Mexico And I 'Meet'?   1
2. Why Mexico?   7
3. How Mexico?   10
4. Why Would We Leave Our Comfortable EU Life   13
   For A Life In A "Developing Country"?
5. Why Mérida?   19
6. What About The Kids?   23
7. Language and School   27
8. How To Move To Mexico With The Correct Visas   30
9. How To Find Somewhere To Live In Mérida   33
10. Household Items And Shopping   43
11. How To Choose A School   50
12. How To Buy A Car   55
13. Medical And Dental Care   60
14. Safety Talk Time   63
15. Real Talk. Finances. How Have We Made It Work?   65
16. Negatives To Living In Mérida   69
17. Final Thoughts   73
    Notes   75
    Where To Find Mexico Cassie   77
    Acknowledgements   79

    Appendices   81

For my family, who are always up for adventure and fun.
Also, for my Tequila girls who have joined us for so much of this brilliant
adventure.
Life is never dull.

Introduction

So you're thinking about moving to Mérida, Yucatán? Well, first off, that's two amazing decisions you're making, moving to my favourite city in the world *and* reading my book.

You're clearly smart people. Good job.

This book is part personal story and part advice. In the book, I'll share my story and my experiences of moving to Mérida with my family. I'll include the toppest of all top tips for making your own move go smoothly as well as some very serious points about how to move to Mérida and set your family up for an amazing time in this stunning city.

While I moved to Mérida with my family, and am largely writing about family life, this book still has plenty to offer for those who are considering moving without children. There are sections that are specifically relevant to people who are considering moving to Mérida with their kids so if you're coming without any, just don't bother reading those sections (or do, of course). You might risk failing the quiz at the end but no biggie. Joke. There's no quiz.

When we first moved to Mérida in 2016 people we met told us there were no foreign families here, that foreigners *retire* to Mérida but they don't come here with their families. Let me correct this here and now: people are absolutely moving to Mérida with their families. Mérida is a wonderful place to bring up children. Pretty much everywhere is family friendly and kids are welcomed in restaurants, cafes, stores, and homes. As a Brit, I have been overwhelmed by how my kids have been embraced (literally and metaphorically) by Mexico. There are foreign families and there are also plenty of Mexican non-Yucatecan families arriving in Mérida too. It's really a cosmopolitan city. We know people from all over Mexico, from North America, from South America, from Europe, from Australasia, from Asia all living in our beautiful Mérida. In 2019, Mérida was ranked, by a business magazine, as the second safest city in North America after Quebec City. It's also considered to be the safest city in Mexico and Forbes ranks Mérida as one of the best Mexican cities to live in.

If you do have children, know that there are great schools in Mérida. There are plenty of activities for the kids, lots of after school classes, and there's always evening fun for kids of all ages.

If you're an adult of any age, never fear, there's plenty for you here too. The restaurant and bar scene in Mérida is thriving (although I write this during the 2020 quarantine so I can't say how it'll look when we come out the other side of this strange time), there are plenty of amazing places to visit, and adventures to be had.

Retirees and snowbirds do make up a large percentage of foreigners to be found in Mérida. Many retirees from Canada and the USA spend significant amounts of time in Mérida and along the Gulf coast exchanging their cold winters for our beautiful, balmy winters.

ONE

How Did Mexico And I 'Meet'?

I'm Cassie. I'm one-quarter of a British family who moved to Mexico in either 2016 or early 2018 depending on how much of my story I feel like sharing on any given day. That sounds weird and evasive, I know, but I promise I'm neither a spy, nor a criminal on the run. We spent six months in Mexico in 2016/17 on an exploratory visit to figure out if we could make a life in Mexico and whether we actually *wanted* to make a life here. During those six months we got so deeply entrenched in both Mexico and Mérida that it absolutely feels as if they should 'count' when discussing our Mexico life even though we only moved here with residency visas under our belts in January 2018.

I have one husband and two young kids (at time of writing they're six and eight) and I'm probably about to be bullied into adopting a cat. I don't like cats. Please don't stop reading even if you now hate me for admitting I don't like cats.

I grew up in the UK with parents who always took my brother and me on fun trips and always told us that the world was our oyster and that we could, and should, do whatever we wanted to do with our lives. Every now and again, though, I'm pretty sure they look at their adult kids and wonder what on earth happened that they wound up with such itinerant offspring (my brother and his family currently live in Belgium but are in the middle of planning a move to an island on the other side of the world). When they said 'the world's your oyster', I think they imagined us as bankers in Rome or at a push, doctors in Canada. I doubt they ever imagined that we would both ditch 'normality' and 'earning good money'. They have taken every single bit of it in their stride though and have never made us feel bad about our decisions.

I think my extremely traditional English education also taught me (entirely by mistake) that it was ok to be different and that 'the path' didn't have to be followed all the way to its expected conclusion of jobs with money and a ton of responsibility. While I was fine with the path itself, in fact I adored 'the path', the destination was never going to be what I wanted. I always knew I wanted to see the world and learn about other cultures rather than stay put in my small town in England.

From Mr. Wilkson, the acerbic French teacher who furnished us with an understanding of existentialist philosophy, to Julian, the English teacher who quit teaching and moved to Ireland for a slower life, the lessons my teachers actively demonstrated while teaching us the syllabus absolutely helped me to learn who I was and helped me shape my own path.

And luckily, I come from a family that expects everything of its offspring but with no set parameters. I also found myself a completely non-conforming husband who also prefers to live outside the normal expectations of society. He didn't think I was weird at all to want to explore and never stay still.

The most common question we get about our move is, 'how do your families feel?' (closely followed by 'how do you make money?' - I'll answer that one at the end of the book). And honestly, they are fine with it. For sure they'd love to live closer and to see us more but Col (my husband) and I both have parents who totally understand the need to travel and explore and to grab life. I mean, they clearly fostered this in us. Col's sister lived in Rwanda and Tanzania for years. Before that, she lived in Japan. And their brother has lived in the Netherlands for over twenty years. We aren't really from families who stay put. Blink and we'll be in a new country. Actually, that's not quite true: we love Mexico and have no plans to leave.

My husband and I met in 2005 in Rwanda. I was working there and he was visiting his sister. When I moved to Ethiopia in early 2006 we decided we weren't ready to end our pretty new relationship so we crazily decided he should come with me. After dating for just eight weeks we moved in with each other in Addis Ababa, a city where I had two friends, and he, none.

We hadn't planned on being quite so hasty but given that we knew almost no one and had very little money, sharing a place seemed more sensible than it might have under other circumstances. And anyway, here we are, 15 years later still very much together despite the fact that within a week of moving in together I got a horrible stomach bug and our bathroom was essentially a partly walled-off corner of the bedroom. Yay for a total lack of privacy in the very early stages of our relationship.

After one year in Addis (surviving bathroomgate), we moved to London, found sensible jobs and got on with life while basically trying to find as many excuses to travel as absolutely possible. Handily for me, my job as a programmes manager for an international development agency meant that I travelled all the time, and that pretty often, Col could join me too.

Only, it turned out this wasn't enough for us. London was awesome; our friends were there, our families were nearby, and the city is obviously fabulous when you're young and free of too much responsibility but it just wasn't enough for either of us. Someone wisely pointed out to me recently that the living in London bit is the anomaly in our lives, *adventuring is our normal.* Living in London, for all its fabulosity, just didn't quench the need for adventure in either of us.

Note to self: get a t-shirt with 'adventuring is our normal' printed on it.

In 2009 we got married in Las Vegas (on purpose). We took 25 of our closest family and friends with us for a crazy Nevada adventure before heading off to Mexico for our honeymoon. We hadn't meant to go to Mexico. I'd wanted to go to Guatemala but somebody, *ahem, cough cough, Col* booked our round trip tickets from London to Las Vegas without checking whether it was possible to get to Guatemala from there. Guess what? It isn't. Not without numerous flights and layovers anyway.

So we went to Mexico.

"M'eh." I thought. "M'eh. I don't wanna go to Mexico. I've been." It's true. I'd spent one whole day in Tijuana as a 14-year-old. So, you know, I didn't really need to go to Mexico again.

Turns out that in Mexico I met the love of my life: Mexico. We spent two glorious weeks in Mexico City, Oaxaca and Chiapas. We drank margaritas, ate guacamole, visited the most fabulous archaeo-logical sites, and drank in (as in inhaled, loved, not got drunk) all Mexico had to offer.

We got home from our honeymoon and, um, decided we'd had enough of being sensible.

We quit our jobs, gave up the lease on our home and went travelling around Asia for six months. We swore we'd never work in London again. Our plan was to go back only briefly after travelling, sort ourselves out, and move straight to Brazil. We'd learn Portuguese and explore South America.

Only we didn't. Despite our Brazil plan, we were both applying for jobs around the world. Jobs were hard to find in 2010 so when we were both offered great jobs, we took them despite the fact that this meant living in London again.

So we went back, started new jobs and had two babies. We bought a house, sold it, bought a bigger one to accommodate children. We got new jobs. We sent the kids to nursery so we could work. Or did we work so we could send the kids to nursery? It felt like a vicious, and never-ending cycle of working to pay for nursery, so we could work so they could go to nursery. It was ridiculous. I was so stressed, and Col was stressed. We were always rushing, we never got to spend quality time with the kids during the week. My job, by this time, was London based but it was more stressful than anything I'd ever done before. It required all the emotional energy I had, then whatever scraps were left were available for the kids and Col. It was a true shocker and absolutely not how either of us wanted our lives to be.

We'd both always talked about going away for six months with the kids to slow things down and to see if we could find a way to live overseas, but we were never ready to go at the same time. One day I'd be fed up with my job but Col would be in a sweet spot, or he'd be fed up and I'd be happy. We never seemed ready to go at the same time.

Until we were.

In late 2015 I was miserable. I remember sitting on an overland train on the way from my office to a work function, the views from the window were all grey and dull: house after house after house, all crammed together, no green and a miserable grey sky. I just thought, 'what are we doing?' I went home and told Col I was done. Surprisingly, he said he was too so we immediately started throwing around countries we thought we could enjoy with the kids.

We couldn't come up with somewhere we both wanted to go so life continued as we kept looking for the 'right' place.

On the way home from nursery one day, the kids and I saw a teenager stab another teenager on a busy street in broad daylight. We were the closest people to the incident. It was obviously horrific (the boy lived, thank goodness). I was an official witness and our older child was fairly traumatised. Everyone thought it was kids punching each other until one boy raised his arm high and we saw the glint of metal.

That night we got serious about making a plan to leave.

For some reason, we had never suggested Mexico up until this point. It just wasn't on our radar, I guess because we'd already been and we were probably unconsciously looking for somewhere new. But now we realised that Mexico was perfect. We'd loved it. We're both obsessed with history, we love learning new languages, we love exploring new places, and we love tequila (!). Col already spoke decent Spanish and I was pretty confident the kids and I could learn. What could be better? So that night we decided we'd go to Mexico for six months and see about changing our future.

TWO

Why Mexico?

O ur adventure that culminated in a permanent move to Mérida began when we knew we wanted to leave the UK and explore somewhere for at least six months. We wanted to have some fun but also to see whether we'd find somewhere that we could live permanently, somewhere we could bring up our kids. We knew what we wanted from that somewhere but we didn't know where that somewhere was.

We wanted somewhere we could all pick up some language skills, somewhere with plenty to do and see, and somewhere where we figured we would stand a fighting chance of understanding a new culture and maybe even fitting in if we were lucky and worked hard.

Then came the fateful evening when the kids were in bed, Col and I were watching tv. I paused the tv and said, 'Mexico'. I don't know why it came to me then but it did. I vividly remember him turning to me and smiling. We both knew that Mexico was the answer we'd been searching for. Sure, we'd been before, but somehow with Mexico that didn't matter. We both actively wanted to go back and explore more.

Mexico has everything we wanted: we could definitely pick up some Spanish in six months, and we would have the option of exploring or staying still and 'living'. We knew we'd be able to rent a house and get to know one place if we wanted to and we knew we'd be able to move around and travel if we wanted to, too.

Oh! It was so exciting! We were starting to have a plan fall into place around us. By nature, I'm an oversharer so I immediately started telling people our plan. I couldn't help myself, how could I keep such a cool idea to myself? And once you tell people you have to do it, right?

I suspect that in Europe, due to distance, we are less concerned with Mexico's reputation than other, closer countries (naming no names). We aren't faced with continuous negative stereotypes and stories about Mexico and Mexicans so the responses we got when we told people were pretty positive. I don't think anyone really asked if we were worried or mad, which I know is something people from the USA often get when they share plans about moving to Mexico. In case you now think Europe is a haven of tolerance and kindness, sadly I have to tell you that we're also perfectly capable of nasty stereotypes and scaremongering.

Col and I did think about Mexico's reputation. Of course we did, but we'd been before and found only incredible kindness and open-ness from people we had met there. In my opinion, this reputation is wrong. Mexico is so, so much more than the few shitty people doing bad things and creating insecurity for others - just like any other country. Mexico is one of the most beautiful countries I've ever visited. It's ecologically diverse, its history is long and fascinating and people are so kind and welcoming. We knew that stereotypes aren't all there are to a country. We chose to focus our energies on the countless positive facets of Mexico. We are from London and almost all of the recent terror attacks on our city had been within a mile or two of our home. We figured we were swapping one poten-tially 'less than perfect' situation for another. Anyone can be 'collat-eral damage' anywhere in the world and we aren't interested in hiding away and never taking a risk. We figure that as long as we don't do dumb shit, stay within the law, and don't go to places known to be dangerous (same rules as anywhere, right?) we are more than likely to be fine.

We've spent time in plenty of places that others might consider to be too dangerous: think Israel at the height of the intifada, Georgia just after a war, and the Democratic Republic of Congo. And let's not forget the doozy, we're from London, somewhere people around the world were scared to visit due to the Northern Ireland crisis of the late twentieth century, and as I mentioned above, the recent terror attacks have all been close to my house.

Six months in Mexico it was. We made the decision that night and set the wheels in motion for renting out our house, quitting jobs, and planning the six-month trip that would turn our lives upside down forever. Wait. I don't actually think we turned our lives upside down, that's not right. I think we put our lives the right way up.

THREE

How Mexico?

I n October 2016 we left London and flew to Oaxaca. We had booked accommodation there for just the first month of our trip, realising that we still had no idea what we wanted from the experience. We chose Oaxaca because we'd had such a brilliant time there on our honeymoon and obviously heading back with two small kids wouldn't be different at all.

On our honeymoon we explored archaeological sites, took long drives, wandered around markets and museums, walked for miles, ate wonderful food, stayed up late, and drank a lot. Of course returning with two tiny kids would be exactly the same!

Idiots. We were idiots. Obviously.

But let's set aside that incredible level of naivety and focus on the good. We quickly re-established our love for Oaxaca and found our daily-routine. We enrolled in a language school and put the kids in kindergarten for the mornings and in the afternoons we explored the city, mainly finding places for the kids to play. We used our weekends to get out into the countryside.

Col wasn't feeling great when we arrived in Mexico. In fact, he'd been ill for the entire planning process in the UK and we almost didn't make the trip (wow, life would have been different) due to his illness. It didn't abate for that first month in Oaxaca and, grasping at straws, he decided (wrongly) that the altitude wasn't helping so he insisted that we move somewhere closer to sea level. While I genuinely didn't want to leave Oaxaca I could see his point that it probably wasn't the right long-term location for us. I also wasn't going to argue with a guy who was ill and had still been brave enough to leave home to explore with me.

Since all my suggestions had been met with firm nos, I left him with the guidebook and told him to get on with finding somewhere for us to go.

Col is always more realistic than me. His head is firmly screwed on and he knew what I couldn't see: we're Londoners. We're from a big city and we do actually like city amenities. He knew we needed the internet to make a living, that we needed schools for our kids (as non-citizens we can't send our kids to Mexican public school), and that we all have a serious sushi addiction that the small mountain town of my dreams wouldn't be able to feed.

So he poured over the Lonely Planet and devised a plan: one month in Tulum (I quickly enrolled us in another Spanish school) and then four months in Mérida. Actually, to begin with, I was adamant that this was the worst Mexico plan ever. I was super pissed off that he wanted to take us to Yucatán. Why on earth would I want to go there? Ugh, Cancun. That's all I knew of Yucatán and I was having none of it. (Of course, now I know that Yucatán is a state, not just the peninsula. I also know now that plenty of people seriously love Cancun and I was being way too judgemental.)

So, my ever-patient husband let me rant a bit and then he showed me photos of sparkling beaches, of archaeological Maya sites, and of colonial Mérida. Damn it. He was right. I hate it when he's right.

We absolutely fell on our feet in Tulum. We found the best language school I've ever studied in, we had a decently priced apartment (still, it was more than we pay in rent for our enormous Mérida house), and living above us was a wonderful Swiss family with two similarly aged kids to ours. We learned Spanish, we hung out on the beach, we explored, and had a full-on great time. We really didn't see the over-priced, trendy hipster hang-out Tulum at all during our month there in 2016. Later, on subsequent visits, I fell slightly out of love with the town as this side of it became more apparent.

We arrived in Mérida at the beginning of December when the 'perfect' weather is well and truly here, we had a house and car and set to work getting to know our new home.

In Mérida, we found our rhythm and we found ourselves. We all fell for this city hard. When March 2017 arrived and it was time to pack up and leave for a final week in Oaxaca before going back to London, we were all devastated. Mérida had welcomed us in and we felt so at home, we were sure we could make a life for ourselves here.

So we left, sad to go but determined to get ourselves back to Mérida, the city that felt like home. It took us nine months but we did it. In January 2018 we said goodbye to the UK and flew back to our new home.

FOUR

Why Would We Leave Our Comfortable EU Life For A Life In A "Developing Country"?

I almost didn't include this section but I think it's important to acknowledge that this is a question we were asked and it's something people may be concerned about in their own decision making process. I said we didn't really face any negative questions but we did get asked this a lot. It wasn't Mexico focused but a general disbelief that we'd want to leave Europe for a less developed country. With the hindsight of 2020, I have the vocabulary to express how I felt in 2016: I can see that this is an inherently Euro-centric point of view cultivated by a system (and an educational system) that promotes this viewpoint. When you've only learned European history or only read European (English) literature and watched movies from Hollywood, how could you think a move to somewhere like Mexico was 'normal'?

Well for my family and me, first of all, 100%, Mexico is not 'less than' anything. Mexico opened its arms and welcomed us in when our own country stopped feeling like home. Mexico has a deep and rich history and culture. Its gastronomy is celebrated and enjoyed around the world, and fabulous people are doing fabulous and innovative things here all the time. We feel beyond grateful and lucky to have stumbled into Mexico and we will always be grateful for the opportunities we've both been given and have made for ourselves here in Mexico.

There are many, many immigrants living in Mexico at the moment, in fact, current wisdom is telling us that there are more people from the USA moving to Mexico every day than going from Mexico to the USA, and much of that southward flow is technically illegal. I'm not from the USA so I won't comment too much but what I will say is that I've met two different types of immigrant to Mexico: those who are here because they actively want to be in Mexico, who love this marvellous culture and want to be part of it and learn from it, and those who are in Mexico because it's cheaper than home. It makes me so sad that people no longer feel that they can afford to live in their own country when they're meant to be from one of the most advanced countries in the world. It also makes me angry (am I allowed to be angry in Mexico's defence?) that people might view Mexico as somewhere to move to just because it's cheap. Too often I see people treating Mexico this way.

OK, enough ranting and back to our personal story.

I've obviously touched on some of the 'whys' but when I stop and reread, I realise that I've talked about the 'push' factors, about what was wrong with the UK, or at least with our family life in the UK. Briefly, we were tired of working so hard to make ends meet, we were tired of having our kids in daycare we could barely afford, we were disappointed in our working environments, and more than a little fed up with the political climate.

We also thrive on adventure and get bored easily, if I'm honest.

But what about the pull factors? The daily grind of London life was our push factor but Mexico had to have the pull factors or we wouldn't be here, or at least wouldn't *still* be here, right?

I guess when we were throwing country names around for so long we were searching for the place with the right 'pull factors'.

We were aware of the potential frustrations and problems that come with living away from the country you know and the rules (written and unwritten) that you just intuitively understand. We knew we had to find somewhere we really wanted to live for the trade-off to be worthwhile.

It might sound selfish to say but for the effort we knew we'd be putting in, we wanted to know it would be worth it. This is why we took six months to explore Mexico and figure out if it was somewhere that could work for us. We didn't want to arrive with all our worldly possessions (basically some children, a load of books, and our passports) and find we had made a mistake and that Mexico just wasn't somewhere we could live.

But the title of this chapter calls Mexico the developing world - is it? What does this term even mean?

According to the IMF (International Monetary Fund), yes, Mexico is a developing country. Technically this just means a country with a less developed industrial base and a lower HDI ranking (Human Development Index) than other countries. Many 'developing countries' actually have a higher growth rate than 'fully developed' countries and they can feel more vibrant, alive, and free on an individual level despite sometimes less than perfect political situations. Here I refer you back to my personal views on my own home country's political situation, *ahem* United Kingdom, sort it out.

A little bit of digging and you find that Mexico is basically considered to be one of the 'most developed developing countries'. It's the second-largest Latin American economy and it's culturally, linguistically, and historically an incredibly rich country. Yes, sure, Mexico's international image may be one of organised crime and danger but that simply isn't the only side to Mexico. I am so grateful, every day, to this fabulous country that has allowed us to make our home here and raise our children to be part of Mexican society.

Also, screw labels. Who gets to pin these labels on countries? I don't like it. Every country has stuff it does brilliantly, stuff it does well, stuff it's fine at and stuff it's less fine at, but the labelling of countries by the capitalist and imperialist current "winners" doesn't have to be accepted and used by us all.

Did you know, for example, that in the latest Expat Insider survey, Mexico comes out top for expat happiness? Eighty-two percent of people who moved to Mexico said they found it easy to make new friends, seventy-seven percent said they found it easy to make local friends, and ninety-two percent said they were happy with their life in general. I don't disagree, Mexico is a great place to live, especially if you're willing to make an effort.

OECD PISA (Programme for International Student Assessment) 2015 report on students' well-being assessed thousands of children around the world. In Mexico, the average life satisfaction (out of 10), was 8.27, whereas the UK average was 6.98. Mexican school kids reported themselves to be some of the happiest children in the world. Obviously, there is a lot more to this research paper than one set of figures but it got my husband and me thinking when we read about it (whilst in Mexico on our six-month exploratory trip). We wanted our kids to be happy at school, right? Obviously. Our kids hadn't yet started formal education in the UK at this point although our older child had a place in a truly excellent local primary school for our return. We were worried about the British educational system, once considered the best in the world (was it? Or was that just the arrogance of a colonialist power? I have no idea). We were worried it was now falling apart.

The emphasis in UK schools has gone from teaching to testing; from fostering a love of learning to testing for exams. Kids and teachers alike, are often unhappy and stressed. Yes. I know this is a generalisation. I promise I know that. We did go home and did put our son into the local state school and we were blown away by the quality of the teaching, the love and care the school provided to the children, and the emphasis they put on growing and creating good people. But even the school couldn't entirely prevent the government's meddling from having an impact. When the government says 'test the children', or 'teach them x or y', the teachers have no choice but to do it.

Truly, one of the few notes in our 'reasons to stay in the UK' list was the schools we'd found for our kids. Our younger child, at this point, was in an urban-forest nursery (kindergarten) that was in our local park. She was basically living a wonderful life, hanging out in the park, learning about nature and having adventures. These schools were what we struggled to leave behind.

But we did leave because we knew that we couldn't make our life decisions based on how we felt about the kids' schools on that day, we had to look at the bigger picture. Truthfully our only real impression of the Mexican education system came from the report I cited. Obviously, like everyone, we want happy, well-adjusted kids. We also know there is more to life than formal schooling. We know that we can provide much of our kids' education at home. They're already almost bilingual. They move in both Mexican society and the immigrant society of Mexico. They remember the UK and running around Stonehenge, but their reality is exploring Maya archaeological sites. They read *The Famous Five* and *Dog Man* at home and Mexican stories at school.

When they're bigger, who knows what our opinion of the Mexican education system will be, but right now, we love the schools our kids are in. We love how the teachers truly love the kids and take a strong interest in every single one of them. Our kids are nurtured and loved at school in Mexico.

Mexico is family-oriented and a great place to bring up kids. What do I see on the street but politeness, kindness, and respect? In the south of the UK we don't habitually say good morning or afternoon to strangers on the street. We avoid eye-contact and get on with our own lives (at least, everywhere I've ever lived has been that way). In Mexico, everyone wishes everyone a good day and our kids are learning to do it too. It's fascinating how even that tiny bit of human interaction can change a perspective on the day. I'm relearning human interaction and my kids are learning to behave this way. It's all they know and I love that. Just the other day, as I walked down my road with my family, a neighbour called out, "buenas tardes, vecinos" (good afternoon, neighbours). She probably has no idea how wonderful that made me feel.

I must add that there is no doubt that for many, life in developing countries is not fun, it is not free, and it is not vibrant, and that sucks. It sucks that people don't have access to the same level of education as my kids, or that they don't get to eat well or have access to first-rate health care or journalism. Of course it does.

FIVE

Why Mérida?

I think you'll all be so disappointed to know that us moving to Mérida really was just chance. As I said above, I'd never even heard of Mérida and when it was suggested to me by Col my first reaction was to shout 'no' and have a little strop. Oooh, I love a little strop.

When Col threw the guide book at me and told me to read more about Mérida, I did as I was told. Mérida sounded ok, if a little flat for my liking. I'm from the flattest region of the UK and although I love my home, it didn't mean I wanted more flatness in my life. Where were my hilly cobbled streets, where were my opportunities to run through fields and climb giant trees in Mérida?

So the truth is that we got to Mérida and I absolutely wasn't convinced by it. We'd had a night in transit when we left Oaxaca and were making our way to Tulum. We were meant to spend three days in Mérida before heading to the beach but 15 hours was enough for us.

I bet that came as a surprise since you're reading a book about moving to Mérida that's written by someone who clearly adores this city. It's true though.

We arrived in early October 2016. The heat and humidity were such a shock after five weeks in Oaxaca where it was hot but not humid. Now I know that October isn't even all that hot for Mérida. We are completely acclimatised and definitely think of October as being the start of the cooler weather. Anyway, for some weird reason, I'd booked us into a hostel rather than a hotel. I guess I forgot that I was a sensible grown-up woman and thought I was still a 20-something party animal. Anyway, we were put in a room that stank of smoke and was right on the patio where all the actual party animals were partying. I did what any sensible parent would do and got our room swapped for one further away BUT it had no A.C., had no private bathroom, and it was small. Suffice to say no one really slept that night.

Over a grumpy breakfast, we decided we really didn't want to spend the weekend in this sweaty hostel in this sweaty town. We called the landlord in Tulum and asked if we could move in two days early. With permission granted, we jumped on a bus and got the hell out.

If you ask my kids (who were two and four at the time) about this experience they'll tell you they remember an amazing adventure where we all slept in a row, that I yelled a lot because they kept jumping from bed to bed. They also remember an amazing breakfast (in reality it was a basic hostel breakfast). They won't remember sweating and sweating and sweating as we walked, with all our stuff, to the bus station, how we couldn't figure out the roads in centro and how we were so excited to get out of Mérida.

Fair to say that Mérida and I did not fall in love at first sight.

Top tip: if you can, try out a location first. If you can't, do your research. Never move blind to a new place if you don't have to. Also, be able to admit that somewhere isn't right for you. Everywhere isn't for everyone.

After an absolutely magical month in Tulum where we frolicked on empty, pristine beaches and studied Spanish every day, we moved to Mérida. While we were excited for a new adventure and to see family (my parents were joining us for a month), I was just sad about leaving the beach and our wonderful language school. I really wasn't sure how I'd feel about being in Mérida and we absolutely didn't have an auspicious introduction to the city.

I felt sick as we found a cab to take us to our new house. I was nervous that there would be no house. We'd handed over money and signed virtual rental papers months previously and were just hoping against hope that the house would be real. I couldn't shake the worry that it could have been a scam. We read so many examples of rental scams, both in England and Mexico that I just couldn't quite relax.

But it was real! And the letting agents even showed up on time. Everything was perfect. The house was nice, the agents seemed nice, the owners of the house had left us a fabulous wealth of information about the house and the local area. Wow.

But then we ate out. We went to a local lonchería because we had no food, we were tired, and didn't want to travel far. It was awful and randomly expensive. I still don't really know why it was that way. I like loncherías and I like panuchos but the ones we had that day were dry and horrid. We went to bed hungry and worried about our upcoming four months in Mérida. At 11 pm the music started. It might as well have been a party in our bedroom it was so loud. It went on until about 3 am. Thank goodness the kids slept through it all. We did not. We were terrified that we'd made a terrible mistake and we'd accidentally moved into the party-zone of Mérida. Thankfully we hadn't and the noise was never repeated.

TOP TIPS:

1. If you can look around before renting a house, do so. If you can't, rent somewhere short term first so you can be sure the area and house work for you.

2. Join local FB groups in the run-up to your arrival. They can be an absolute wealth of knowledge but be aware that not everyone in the groups will be totally

lovely. Use search functions in groups because many questions will have been asked many times before.

Anyway. From this moment on, Mérida and I began our love affair. We explored Centro, we threw ourselves into checking out the free cultural activities and eating everything the city offered us. I found a language school for me, we found a small school for the kids, we met other families making their lives here and settled down fast. We also got out of town as often as possible, checking out cenotes, beaches, archaeological sites, and nearby small towns. We were absolutely in our element.

That's my introduction to Mérida story. We spent four months in the city and when it was time to return to the UK we realised we didn't want to go home. We felt settled and Mérida felt like home.

SIX

What About The Kids?

I wanted to start this chapter by saying 'everyone says the kids will be fine' but then I realised that is a blanket statement that isn't necessarily true at all. It really depends on where you're going, how old the kids are, and who your kids are.

Let me tell you about my kids and how they coped. We have two kids with extremely different temperaments. Our older child, who was three when we started discussing spending time overseas, had been an extremely demanding baby and toddler. He wasn't the type of child who reacted particularly well to massive change. We had tried a few European holidays with him when he was tiny and found they were more stressful than we expected them to be. We decided to hold off on long-haul travel until he was big enough to under-stand and better cope with new situations. Our second child is far more laid back and accepting of everything life throws at her so we quickly realised that as soon as child number one was ready for a life of exploration, we could go.

By the time he was four, we could have a proper conversation with him and explain about holidays and temporary changes. I say that but it still wasn't easy. He was pretty upset about our first move to

Mexico in 2016 but he didn't have the emotional maturity or language to tell us. He used his actions to show us instead. The most memorable has to have been when he locked the Spanish nanny in the garden - we'd hired her specifically to help the kids get used to hearing Spanish and he was having none of it.

He was adamant he didn't want to learn Spanish and that he *wouldn't* learn Spanish (he's now, aged eight, practically bilingual, making puns in Spanish, correcting his parents and desperate to pick up as many languages as he can, by the way). I remember walking with him in London and suggesting that he at least learn to understand '¿quieres un helado?' in case anyone asked if he wanted an ice-cream. How sad to miss out on ice-cream because he was too stubborn to learn.

We hired a Spanish nanny for one day a week. The little one fell in love with her. The bigger one, not so much. He was angry (I guess scared and nervous) and tried his hardest to have nothing to do with her. We had to breathe deep and remember that he was only four, we were turning his little life upside down, taking him away from his friends, family, parks, toys, everything he knew. And he had no idea what to expect.

We tried constantly to talk to him, to show him photos and videos, to get him excited about Mexico. We got nursery staff to talk about Mexico too. They were fabulous. We asked him about his feelings, asked him to try and tell us how he felt. We used colours, we used weather words to try and give him a language he could manage to express his feelings. But he really isn't a touchy-feely kinda kid. He didn't want to talk about his feelings. He asked if they had Spiderman in Mexico and then he stopped talking.

When I came home to find he'd locked the nanny in the garden we realised he really was unhappy. Now, a few years later, we definitely laugh at this incident but at the time it was just devastating to realise that our small boy couldn't express his obvious worries and fears except through anger and acting-out.

The nanny, by the way, spoke to the kids in Spanish and English. We weren't expecting her to achieve much with one day a week, we just wanted our kids to be used to the sound of Spanish. The small boy was eventually won over when she taught him how to say 'fart' in Spanish (it's pedo, if you're interested).

Unexpectedly, he was fine within moments of arriving in Mexico. He was excited, and back to his usual happy self except for the odd moment. The two-year-old was obviously absolutely fine with everything. She was far too small to have real opinions about where she was. She just needed to be with her family.

And, when it came to returning to the UK in April 2017, our son actively didn't want to go home and played up in the same way. In our last week (spent in an Airbnb in a mountain village outside Oaxaca) he pulled some ridiculous stunts including almost exploding the house by putting dry leaves in the boiler (I must add that he obviously had NO idea what the consequences of this could have been). He dropped toy cars between the sliding patio doors and drew on the floor. Luckily we managed to fix everything.

In my situation, everyone definitely assumed our kids would be fine but as you can see from the stories above, it wasn't easy or all plain sailing.

When we told the kids we were moving back to Mexico permanently we didn't have any big reaction from either kid. Both knew what they were moving to so felt confident with the move. They were both sad to leave their schools and their friends but they weren't scared like they were the first time. They'd experienced life in Mexico, could picture where we were going, and knew they already had friends there.

I am writing in mid 2020. We have now spent three years in Mexico. That's half our daughter's life. She's celebrated four out of her six birthdays here, something she's very proud of. Our son still likes to tell people he was born in England but I know that he is working out his identity. He is very proud of the fact that he speaks such good Spanish and that he lives in Mexico. It's fascinating to see that he even prefers to speak Spanish with the English teachers at his school. He reads in English but writes in Spanish. Both kids tell me that they know they're British but they don't remember so much about 'home' so it kind of feels like a dream to them now. In the summer of 2020 we had planned to go back to the UK for a visit, but the pandemic kinda got in our way a bit. We absolutely think it's important that our kids retain links to their birth country and will take a trip back as soon as it's safe to do so. I find it fascinating, by the way, that I feel guilt if I refer to the UK as 'home'. I wonder if that's normal.

In 2019 we took a trip to the USA. Within an hour of arriving we saw an advertisement for a restaurant that sold tacos. I've never heard such relief from my son as when he saw this and said, "Oh, thank goodness, they have tacos here". And recently I offered the kids the choice of fish tacos or fish and chips (remember, this is basically a national dish for us Brits). They looked at me as if I was completely mad and demanded tacos with their fish.

I can't wait until they're a bit older and start having history classes at school. I feel strongly that it's our job to ensure our children know the history of our country and continent while school will teach them Mexican history. I'm so aware of how my own education was Euro-centric and I totally understand that it isn't possible to teach children a true world history but I really am excited for my kids to start out with a less Euro-centric worldview than I was given. I've had to work hard, and I continue to work hard, to widen my worldview. Before coming to Mexico, I knew next to nothing about the history of this country.

SEVEN

Language and School

P eople say kids pick up languages super easily, that they're like sponges. I'd probably have said the same a few years ago but I'm a little more circumspect now, having taken my basically monolingual children and deliberately dumped them in an all Spanish environment.

When we arrived in 2018, my kids were not entirely clueless about speaking Spanish or Mexican schools, having spent a while in school here already. We enrolled both in kindergarten and hoped for the best. We deliberately chose a non-bilingual school because we wanted the kids to pick up Spanish as quickly as possible. Our kids weren't the first non-Mexicans at the school and the teachers who could speak English were very kind with the children and with us (because, yes, adults also have to be able to manage school interactions, which truthfully, can be exhausting).

Obviously the children were very quiet to begin with, it was harder to make friends without much Spanish, and classes were less interesting when they didn't really understand what was going on. Handily for us, our school was very much focused on learning through play so getting to grips with activities was easier than it would have been had they been expected to sit and write all day long.

While our son had no English speaking friends in his class (and to date never has), our daughter has, each year, had at least two other English speakers in her class. I am in no doubt that this has slowed her full immersion as she could rely on her friends to translate for her.

Our son is a natural communicator. He has always been this way so for him, it was difficult to have his "superpower" removed. Being unable to express himself in Spanish, he felt lost and extremely frustrated, which of course, then had an impact on his behaviour. He couldn't be himself and, as such, started playing up and refusing to cooperate at school. We hired a tutor and for two terms she came twice a week to work with the kids, focusing just on giving them confidence in Spanish. She was an enormous help then and is still absolutely beloved by my kids.

School had to call us a few times about our son's behaviour because he just wasn't settling in. It was maybe the second time they called that we realised we needed a different tack. In the car our son rarely opens up as he prefers to read so I decided to walk home from school with him. He and I had some of our best conversations during these walks. We would buy ice cream and talk all the way home. One-on-one time is often hard to come by in our busy world but it turned out it was just what he needed. I told him how I was feeling, that it was hard for me, too, to live in Spanish, that I was struggling with some of the school interactions as well. I truly think it made a huge difference to know that his mum was also struggling at times.

TOP TIP: Remember that kids might need 'permission' to show you that they're struggling. Do open that discussion with your children, give them permission to tell you how they're feeling and acknowledge their feelings. It'll make all the difference.

After two years in school both kids are doing fine. They aren't yet entirely bilingual but they are fluent and are educationally on par with their peers.

I write this during coronavirus times so school is online, which means I know more about what is going on than ever before. The one thing that really stands out to me is that the teachers are correcting all the kids' use of gender and agreement, not just the foreign kids. It seems that seven and eight-year-olds aren't really expected to have it all perfect yet. I guess it's comparable with English speaking kids not yet having all their irregular verbs correct at the same age.

Of course, there will be kids who are entirely bilingual quickly, and there will be kids who struggle more to acquire the second language but everyone will get there. Children are still learning their first language when they're under ten. My kids are fascinated by the fact that despite my obviously larger vocabulary in Spanish, their Spanish is far more fluent than mine and they sound Mexican where I can only dream of sounding like them. Of course I have a better vocabulary. I'm an adult. I need more words and I have more words in English. It makes sense.

EIGHT

How To Move To Mexico With The
Correct Visas

Upon arrival in Mexico, visitors from countries that don't require a visa are generally given 180 days in the country. While many people do live here on this tourist allowance, leaving every six months to renew, this is absolutely not recommended. I don't recommend it for both practical and ethical reasons. Practically, I'd hate to live with the worry that I could be kicked out of somewhere I considered to be my home at any point. As immigration services get more advanced there are more and more stories of computerised systems alerting the authorities to people doing this and then handing out shorter visas when they try to re-enter after a short trip to Belize.

For me, more importantly, are the ethical reasons to not live this way. I come from a rich country that doesn't always treat immigrants well. I feel very strongly that the arrogance my country shows can not be replicated or represented in my actions. People in my country get angry about "illegal" immigrants and as such, I absolutely want to show my respect and gratitude to the country that has given me a home and not come across as an arrogant individual who thinks she's above the rules.

So, we followed the rules and applied for residency for the four of us. It isn't an especially fun process, and you do need to have a decent amount of savings if you plan on living in Mexico without a work visa. As a family, we were advised by the Mexican Embassy in London to have just one adult apply for temporary residency from our home country (for the process has to be begun outside of Mexico) and have the other three apply for family unity visas once we were in Mexico.

There are two visas for people wanting residency in Mexico: temporary and permanent. Both must be applied for outside of Mexico.

Temporary: one year is given in the first instance and this can then be renewed in Mexico for one, two, or three years. You can request work permissions on a temporary visa but they are not given automatically.

With a temporary visa you can come and go from Mexico as often as you like. You cannot vote, take part in anything political (including protests by the way), cannot own land or property 50km from the coast or 100km from a land border without a fideicomiso.

Permanent: If you have enough funds you can apply for a permanent visa from the outset. This gives more rights (you can work) but still aren't allowed to own property. In addition, you forfeit the temporary visa right to bring in a foreign plated car.

After four years on a temporary visa you can exchange your visa for a permanent one. Retirees or people with close family ties to Mexico can apply for a permanent visa immediately.

To use my husband's guide to acquiring residency in Mexico, head to mexicocassie.com or read it in the appendices at the end of this book. I've been told it's the most thorough and detailed guide available. The most important thing to remember, if you're going to do your own process, is check, double check and triple check everything. And be prepared to be sent away from INM offices if there is even the tiniest error in your paperwork.

We found almost without fail, that people working in INM were incredibly friendly and helpful but their hands were tied by the system. For example, they'd help figure out the exact right text to write on forms and allow you to change it at their desk but if a translated copy of a document had a number out of place, you'd be out on your ear!

Check the appendices for helpful vocabulary.

NINE

How To Find Somewhere To Live In Mérida

I f you want to move to Mérida you'll obviously need somewhere
to live. Mérida, for newcomers, essentially splits into three
options: centre, north, privadas. Of course, this is a simplistic view
of the city but it's fine for now. There are many, many areas to the
city but these are the three that most newcomers generally consider.
You'll also need to know if you're planning on renting or buying,
buying and renovating, or even buying land and building.

Centro: mainly colonial houses, walking distance to restaurants and
cultural events.

North: the 'good' schools, malls, international style restaurants, large
supermarkets.

Privadas: primarily in the north and outside the periferico (ring
road), these are gated communities (of varying sizes), often preferred
by people with children as the larger ones have play spaces and kids
can ride bikes safely.

When we first decided to come to Mérida, we didn't want to live in
the north of the city. We wanted to live in the centre. We thought it
would give us a more exciting and lively experience of Mexico if we

lived right in the heart of everything. Thus far we've had three houses in Mérida: one slightly south of Centro in La Ermita, one just off Paseo Montejo and one slightly north of Centro.

House Number 1: La Ermita, Centro

Living in La Ermita was just wonderful. We rented a modern house there. We had a big pool and big garden and two plazas within minutes of our house. We would take the kids to play every evening and always see the same people. We could walk to a large supermarket and Centro was just about within walking distance. However, we found that we were far from modern conveniences like the malls and it was much longer to get to the beach than we imagined. The house was on a main bus route and we never found life particularly quiet in that house. We were plagued by mosquitos constantly thanks to neighbours who weren't keeping their yards properly.

House Number 2: Near Paseo Montejo, Centro

Our next house was in a more 'prosperous' part of town and this time we chose a refurbished colonial house. It was fun being able to walk to Centro and to the restaurants on Montejo and Santa Lucia. We didn't enjoy the lack of parking or still being on a busy road. For us, this location also lacked the sense of community we felt in La Ermita.

House Number 3: Buenavista

Now we live further north in a large house that isn't colonial. It has its idiosyncrasies, for sure, but it is on a quiet street, it's closer to the modern stores and schools, and the activities our kids want to do, we have windows that open, and a house that barely leaks. There still isn't the community we felt in La Ermita but we know our neighbours and love our road.

You may well be renting sight unseen for the first months of your time in Mérida. This, of course, makes things harder and is why we wound up with three months in a house with no airflow at all. I recommend renting for a maximum of three months if you can't check out a house in person. Once you arrive, start looking around for your longer term home.

Where to look for your house: from overseas you can either hire someone to look for a house for you or you can use airbnb to get yourself to Mérida and look for a house yourself. If you're looking to move to Mérida it's always worth asking about deals for longer term stays with Airbnb rather than taking the first price offered as people are always keen on having longer-term tenants and a guaranteed income.

There are plenty of rental agents who speak English who can help you find a place to live. If you speak Spanish my recommendation is always to go to a local agent who may be more likely to know what's happening outside of the expat circles and who won't be charging expat prices. There are, of course, benefits to the English speaking agents: they're often more likely to have an online presence and to offer the type of support you may need when arriving in a new country. When we moved back to Mérida we asked some agents to help us find a house outside of Centro. They told us that there really weren't houses to rent in the north in our price range. This was utter nonsense and it would have made far more sense for them to just say that they only worked in Centro but they wanted our business so they told this untruth.

Things to think about when house hunting:

- It gets very hot in Mérida so airflow is important. People say that a house on the north-south axis gives the best breeze and I would agree with this.
- Can you cope without a pool or A.C? Prices will be much lower without them but will you be happy?
- Do windows open? Is the street so busy you won't want to have open windows due to traffic pollution?
- How light is the house? Is it very light but this means the house is constantly hot?
- Smell: some of the newly remodelled houses have a damp

35

concrete smell to them. This eventually fades but are you ok with it?

- Water pressure: some new or renovated houses have extra pumps, others don't. Check and only take what you're happy with. Most have just a tinaco (water tank) on the roof. A basic pump sends the water up there from the mains. The pressure comes from the water descending into the house.
- Rain and leaks. Rain is a serious business here in Mérida. Our first house came with an instruction booklet that made a big thing of the fact that the house didn't leak. We didn't understand why this was until we moved into our second home and found the regular leaking spots.
- Do you need furnished or not?
- Not all houses allow pets.
- Length of lease - a few months is fine through Airbnb or for some of the expat rented homes but a regular Mexican lease is generally for a year or two at a time.
- If you're renting you may be asked for a guarantor and if you don't have one, you will probably be asked to provide a larger deposit. This is normal.

So now you know what to look for but how do you even get inside to consider these issues? Well, you have options. As I said above, there are plenty of realtors (estate agents) who will send you options online. You can also use Facebook groups, vivanuncios.com.mx and Airbnb online.

> **TOP TIP: Any agent can show any house in Mérida so if you have a preferred agent and then see a house advertised with someone else, it's worth asking your agent to show it to you.**

Once you're in Mérida, if you feel brave you can head to the neighbourhood in which you think you'd like to live and just walk or drive around. You'll see which houses are for rent or sale as they'll have big signs outside with a phone number listed. Call or text for details. That's how we found our home. I saw a place near my kids' school and texted for more information. The realtor told me it wasn't what I was looking for but she had another place she thought I might like. She was right. I did. We all did and now we've lived in it for three years.

You'll find useful house hunting vocabulary in the appendix.

BILLS/SERVICES

Often when you rent from a foreign realtor (someone set up specifically to deal with immigrants) then your bills will be included in your rent, or they'll be paid and then you'll be charged. Airbnb rentals, even long term, can include the bills. If you're renting a 'regular' home in Mérida, obviously you'll be paying your own bills.

Ways to pay bills:

- Pay your bills online if you have a Mexican bank account
- In a service office
- Pay in one of the following stores: Oxxo, GoMart, Aki, Coppel, Ahorro, Willies, Bunosusa. Just present your bill to the cashier and pay.

My family rents a house. Our water and electricity bills remain in our landlord's name, which is fairly common. These documents are still accepted as our proof of address, which might seem weird but is perfectly normal.

WATER - JAPAY (Junta de Agua Potable y Alcantarillado de Yucatán): there is a meter in every house (generally) and bills are paid every two months. Mains water is not dangerous and will not kill you, but people do not drink it if they have other options. The mineral content in the water is too high and apparently, over time, will give you kidney stones. People have varying views on how they deal with water. We have a water filter built in. We haven't risked drinking the water though, as we don't know how good the system is. My husband tells me that this filter has probably meant our washing machine is healthier than it might otherwise be.

We brush our teeth in regular tap water, wash in it (I know some people think it's too hard even for hair washing), and will boil food in it if it doesn't absorb water but we wouldn't drink it or use it to cook something like pasta. We absolutely do wash our fruit and veg in it. Others don't even do this and either use a special solution or filtered water for washing food. Most people, from what I can gather, do not give their animals tap water to drink.

Pozo water: this is well water. Many homes in Mérida have their own well. This water tends to fill pools rather than feed house systems. Not all homes have their own pozos though. We had to get a water truck to fill up our pool when we moved in and now we use mains water to top it up when we need to. It isn't ideal but it is what it is.

Drinking water: This can be delivered in 20 litre garafons (large plastic bottles). Cristal and E-pura are the two main delivery options. You can also pick up garafons at Oxxos and supermarkets. Be aware that you need to have empty garafons to swap for full ones and many supermarkets won't let you take that initial garrafon but Oxxo and Six will. A deposit is required par garrafon. Ask your neighbours who delivers water and when to your area.

ELECTRICITY - CFE (Comisión Federal de Electricidad): many people choose to add solar panels to their homes to bring down electricity prices. In the summer months, Mérida homes receive a small subsidy on electricity because it's so hot here. If you don't use too much electricity, bills aren't too painful. If you do go into 'alto consumo' (high consumption) then you are charged more per KW. Having just gone into it for the first time ever, we are pretty upset in our house! Once you're in alto consumo it takes a year to get out of it. This is also something to consider when renting a house. You don't want to be paying for the previous tenants' high consumption.

GAS - Abimerhi or Zeta Gas: you'll quickly get used to the Zeta Gas jingle as trucks drive through the neighbourhood. Gas is generally stored in tanks on the roof (ensure any house you want to rent is set up for this as not all are) and you call to get the gas replaced. Although this may sound odd and slow, actually we find that the truck shows up within an hour or two of you calling so as long as you're aware, it's ok. We always try to remember to check before Christmas and when there are big storms warnings.

GARBAGE COLLECTION - Sana, Corbase, Pamplona, Servilipias: For garbage collection, find out which company serves your area. If the estate agent can't tell you, ask your neighbours. We pay via the website and garbage is collected three times a week. The collection is generally at night, especially if you live in Centro, where the garbage trucks aren't allowed on the roads during busy daytime hours. Our service comes any time between 7pm and 1am and the guys always yell out in the hope of receiving a tip or a snack.

RECYCLING - recycling is possible in Mérida although it isn't as simple as it is in the UK, or I assume other European countries or the USA/Canada/Australia. You have options if you want to recycle (please do).

- You can leave most recycling outside your house and people will come and take it either for personal use or to return themselves for the small monies it provides (glass and plastic particularly).
- Take things to the Punta Verde recycling points around town (many use the Slow Food Market on a Saturday) and Plaza Akropolis in Fraccionamento Las Americas.

INTERNET - TELCEL, IZZI, TEL MEX - you'll hear horror stories about all the options. My husband and I both work online and from home so we need good internet. We have Izzi in our house and we've always been impressed with the speed and service provision. It almost never goes down. Our router was fried by lightning in a storm once and within two days we were delivered a new one. When the internet does fail we receive a text message as soon as it's clear it'll be more than a few minutes telling us that Izzi is aware of the problem and that they're working on it.

CELL PHONE - TelCel, Movistar or AT&T are the three cell options. TelCel is the most popular. If you want to use your phone from overseas, ensure it's unlocked.

I have a Telcel chip in an unlocked phone. When you first arrive in Mexico just pick up a sim card at any Oxxo and then buy pay-as-you-go credit when needed. I have never had a problem with my monthly $200 peso paquete that allows me unlimited calls, Facebook, Instagram and WhatsApp. There are options for shorter paquetes too.The data isn't unlimited but I've never gone over my limit, and I'm a pretty prolific phone user. The brilliant thing is that even this pay-as-you-go option works in the USA and Canada so if you're heading north of the border just ensure you're topped up before you leave and you're good to go.

You can recharge your credit in Oxxo, most supermarkets, Telcel stores, and even online. It's also possible to set up an automatic recharge although I haven't chosen to do this myself.

Top Tip: "Un paquete de telcel sin limite doscientos pesos, por favor" - translation "a telcel 'sin limite' (the name of the packet I get) $200 pesos, please.

I am renowned for forgetting that I need to recharge my credit but brilliantly, Telcel will allow you to use the phone without credit for a short while. Do beware though, that costs for this are deducted from your next paquete purchase, which probably then means your next paquete won't last as long as you expect. I've relied on this service soooooo many times!

It is possible to get a phone and contract if you're a resident but I genuinely don't think it's necessary or cheaper than an unlocked phone and monthly paquetes. The only reason to get a contract would be if you need to use your phone in other countries around the world but given how easy it is to get a local sim card in most countries, I don't really see this as a benefit anymore.

TV - most people I know watch Netflix, Amazon Prime, Sky. People often choose to have a VPN (Virtual Private Network) to allow them to watch tv from their home countries. A VPN essentially hides your location and allows you to tell the internet you're in a different country thus allowing you to watch tv from home.

Household Help: Many people have household help. It's very common to have a housekeeper, cleaner, pool-person, gardener, cook or nanny. We have a cleaner who comes once a week for four - five hours. Often someone will 'come with your house'. You can choose to keep them or not, but please do remember that it isn't always easy for them to find new work or for you to find new staff you like and trust. If you do need someone, ask your neighbours and friends for recommendations. As a baseline, we pay our cleaner $300 pesos for four - five hours of work a week. We also pay her when she's sick and when we don't need her when we're away. We are about midrange in cleaner salaries, I think. We pay extra when we ask for more work, when people come and stay, for example.

If your cleaner stays with you over a meal time it's the 'done thing' to either provide food or give money for food. We don't tend to eat more than snacks while our cleaner is with us, but she knows she can help herself to anything in the kitchen. If I make myself a snack I always offer her the same, and I always begin the day telling her what food we have so she really knows she's welcome to it.

Alguinado - anyone who hires Mexican workers needs to know about the alguinado. While this is often referred to as the 'Christmas tip', it emphatically isn't a tip or a bonus but a legally required additional payment. Of course, when staff are paid informally it can be ignored but I highly recommend paying it. This additional payment is meant to be equivalent to 15 days wages and is designed to help people cover Christmas costs. It's payable before 20th December. I generally ask my cleaner if she'd prefer it before buen fin (Mexican

Black Friday) or Christmas as the buen fin sale is when people often begin to prepare for Christmas.

My family has never spent a lot of money on clothes or pretty shiny things. Our house is not beautiful but it's comfortable. We loathe our sofa, by the way. We bought it when we first got here and were trying to save money. We were feeling sick about all the things we needed since we left almost everything we owned in the UK and so we bought cheap. We have regretted it every single day. We try not to regret things but this sofa is awful! We bought it for $5000 pesos in Elektra. Don't do that if you don't have to. We always say it'll be the first thing we replace when we finally have cash, and then whenever we have a bit of spare money we choose to travel instead of splurging on a sofa.

TEN

Household Items And Shopping

I f you're moving to Mérida then you'll need to make some many decisions. Do you know if you are:

1. Moving into a fully furnished place
2. Shipping all your stuff here
3. Starting from scratch

New residents to Mexico are granted a one off tax free allowance called "Menaje de casa" to bring in household items to help set up home in Mexico. I believe items must be over six months old and you must be in possession of your residency card, not just a visa sticker in the passport. We weren't told about this option when we moved here so just came with excess luggage.

Top Tip: Find moving boxes that are exactly the dimensions of the largest baggage permitted on the aeroplane. It's far easier to pack a box than a suitcase to make the most of your allowance.

Coming from Europe without a company paying moving fees, we opted to leave pretty much everything behind and start again. Mérida is a decent sized city and there are plenty of options for every price band. If you want international brands there are department stores such as Chapur and Liverpool, and even Costco, where you can fit out your house beautifully. There are also plenty of designer furniture stores in plazas in the north of the city and some incredible artists to be found who make wonderful bespoke furniture or restore old items.

At the lower price end are places such as Elektra and Coppel where everything is perfectly functional. Supermarkets also sell pretty much everything you need to outfit your house, including sofas, beds, white goods, and even motorbikes.

My family had a pretty modest budget so we shopped around and were careful with what we bought. I'll outline, below, where we bought our big ticket items.

Top Tip: There are plenty of sales in stores, Black Friday does exist in Mexico, it's called Buen Fin and lasts for a weekend.

Kitchen: We bought all our white goods in Soriana in the sales. The value was actually very good and we haven't been unhappy with anything. We got international brands at good prices.

Oven: as a European I was surprised to find that ovens here don't often have grills built in. You need to buy what's confusingly called a 'toaster oven' if you want to grill stuff. I haven't, but I still might. The majority of ovens are gas both top and bottom. Gas in Mérida isn't piped into the house but stored on the roof. I desperately miss my UK oven with its built-in grill and convection oven because I find it so hard to bake with gas. I was a scone-master in the UK but here, not once in three years have I successfully made scones that rise (grumble grumble).

Bedrooms: We had our beds and bedside tables made by a local carpenter. I regret it because the quality just isn't as high as the carpenter promised us. One bed broke the moment it was sat on. The carpenter did come to repair it immediately, but we still weren't very thrilled. We bought most of our mattresses at Super Colchones and later bought more at Soriana - we were happy with the quality and price of both.

> **TOP TIP: If you're coming from Europe, beds are different sizes from those in Mexico. My single bed sheets only just fit on single beds here but all the double bedding I brought with us is useless. Bedding in Mexico is a weird thing. It can be hard to find soft 100% cotton unless you're willing to spend an absolute fortune. I also find that whatever I've bought here in Mexico just doesn't quite fit perfectly either and nor do the sheets a friend bought for me in Canada. I don't know what it is with sheets and beds, maybe they just hate me. North Americans, you can bring bedding; Europeans, don't bother!**

Living Room: I already admitted to our sofa fiasco. Don't be us. We had bookshelves and tables made by the same carpenter who made the beds. I also regret that. There are some wonderful carpenters and artists around, unfortunately this guy was not one of them. Ask around, get recommendations, check work. Everything we ordered from our carpenter arrived late, badly made, unsanded, with marks and with holes filled with pink putty. He had the audacity to try and claim this was "rustic". How we laughed. Sigh. He gave me cheese as an apology. I'm a sucker for cheese, it's true, but it doesn't mean I don't shake my head in sadness every time I see my poor falling apart table or my daughter reminds me her bed has a broken slat.

We absolutely wanted to use a carpenter and support an individual rather than buy from national or international chain stores. However, I'd do more research than we did last time if we were to do this again. My husband asks me to add here the fact that leaving wood to sit for two years before using it is simply beyond the budget of many carpenters, which is why wood splits.

If you want a TV, check out the electronics sections of the supermarkets as well as Costco or Sam's. There are always good deals to be had.

Bathrooms: If you're moving to an older, unrenovated house in Mérida, be aware that toilet paper needs to go in a dustbin, not down the loo (toilet). Many people get around this by buying a bumgun / douche. This is obviously also a more sustainable option but doesn't work if your water pressure is dire (ahem, my house). More modern houses and refurbished houses often have better systems and therefore can cope with toilet paper being flushed.

Food Shopping

There are numerous supermarkets and convenience stores dotted around Mérida. You'll never struggle to find somewhere to shop.

Supermarkets/Grocery Stores: Wal-Mart, Chedraui, Superarma, Soriana, Super Akí, Bodega Aurrera, Willies.

While all of the stores sell pretty much the same stock, there are some differences and everyone has their preferences. My specific choices are:

Wal-Mart City Center (confusingly, this is a plaza in the north of the city) - great for fresh fruit and vegetables.

Chedraui Norte Selecto - a good all-rounder.

Chedraui Selecto Kalia - good for imported goods. Great cheese counter. Probably the most 'upmarket' option in Mérida.

Super Akí - we have found their world beer section to be surprisingly good.

Soriana - I love a Soriana shop. Their fruit and vegetables tend to be good, as does the fresh bread (cakes, we have found to be terrible).

At the cheaper end of the spectrum are:

Bodega Aurrera - cheaper supermarket. It's owned by Wal-Mart.

Willies - you tend to find this store in smaller pueblos. Don't expect to find many imported goods here.

Wholesale: We have both Costco and Sam's Club. Both require membership to shop here but they're great for buying in bulk and for finding international branded items.

Top Tip: Bag packers and the people helping load your car are not paid by the store, give them a tip.

Convenience stores: You can hardly fail to notice the red and yellow Oxxo stores that are pretty much taking over Mexican roadsides. These stores sell drinks, snacks and the basic foodstuffs. You can pay bills, top up your phone, and deposit money in accounts at Oxxo.

Tienditas: Of course, there are always local independent 'tienditas' everywhere, too. I equate these with English corner shops. They are small, independent, and sell the basics needed by people in the area.

Markets: There are plenty of markets in Mérida. The biggest is Lucas de Galvez in the centre of town. I love just wandering around and making random purchases as well as going with my list of needs. If you eat meat, I recommend castacan (pork belly) from the market. The best quesillo (Oaxaca cheese) in Mérida, in my opinion, is found in this market. The fruit and veg are great quality, and the spice selection is always good.

Other markets: Santa Ana and Santiago are renowned for having decent markets too. Most areas have their own markets, and you'll also find small fruit and veg stalls along the side of the road. There are butchers' stores offering local and north Mexican style meats around the city.

The Slow Food Market is an organic and slow market held every Saturday. This is a popular market with locals and newcomers and is a great spot to pick up delicacies. If you're used to a local farmers' market, this is your Mérida equivalent.

Zero-Waste Market tends to be held once a month at varying locations around the city. Be sure to take your own containers and bags as they are serious about their zero-waste ethos.

Feria Vegana - a market for vegan options that is generally held at the train museum. You'll find vegan food stalls, classes and fun at these events. Held at the train museum usually.

Sustainable stores: Fantastically, Mérida has an abundance of sustainable, zero-waste stores and more seem to be popping up all the time. All of the below can be found on Facebook.

- Mr. Tofu - Vegan Supermarket. Avenida 1H 98, Colonia México Norte
- Ay Granel - sells loose products, grains and oils, etc. Take your own containers. Calle 74 400, Fraccionamiento Las Américas
- Ya'axtal - eco-store. A few branches around town
- Monique's Bakery - vegan yoghurt, healthy breads, focus on fermented food, probiotics and more. Calle 79 #191A entre 36 y 38 Montes de Ame
- Colectivo Muul Meyaj - crafts and food products. Calle 45 # 499 X 58 Y 60 Barrio de Santa Ana
- Vida Sustenable - health food shop. Calle 55 #548 A x 70 y 72 Centro
- Expendio de Leche Pura de Vaca Milk based products. Calle 69 #542 por 66 y 68 Col. centro
- Puras Cosas Buenas - health store and restaurant. Avenida José Díaz Bolio 103
- Aromas Organicas Y Naturales - food, personal hygiene and cleaning products - on Facebook)
- Woolis Market - new in 2020. Farm delivery. Find on Facebook.
- Kuxtal Market - new in 2020. Farm delivery. Find on Facebook.

- Green Shine - refills of cleaning products - x 22 y 20, Calle 21 104 B, Chuburná de Hidalgo, 97205 Mérida, Yuc.

Speciality Stores and International Cuisine: There is very little you can't find in Mérida in the way of food products. We have vegan stores and health stores as noted above, there is an Asian speciality store, a Lebanese store, there are delis that specialise in importing coveted food items too.

Restaurants: You can find almost every cuisine catered for in Mérida: from Yucatecan (because, yes, the region absolutely has its own unique cuisine), to 'Mexican', to Japanese and Korean, to Italian, we can get it. We have international chain restaurants, incredible individual restaurants, and local chain restaurants too. You won't lack for anything, except maybe good Chinese food!

Banking In Mérida

All the regular international banks are represented in Mérida as well as Mexican banks. It is rarely free to withdraw money from your overseas bank unless you go directly to that bank (HSBC and Santander, for example). Banks charge their own random amounts for withdrawal.

Residents can open bank accounts and this can be useful to do as then you can pay bills online and shop online with mercadolibre. We opted for HSBC as it was the most streamlined of all the processes we considered.

Setting up standing orders can be extremely annoying and time consuming but is possible, you just need patience.

ELEVEN

How To Choose A School

I f you're going to be citizens then your kids can attend public school should you so wish. If you're not citizens, rather "only" residents, you'll have to send your kids to private schools if you aren't homeschooling. These come in all shapes and sizes in Mérida so you'll need to figure out what sort of school you want for your kids. There is a 'right school' for everyone.

- Do you want bilingual education? Teaching in Spanish? Teaching in English? Half and half?
- How traditional do you want your school to be?
- Do you want Montessori for learning through play?
- What are your views on homework and uniforms?
- What about the school ethos? Some schools are very strong on sports while others focus more on social growth.

Figure out what you want and then ask around, visit schools, get a feel for them. You must know though, that Mérida is growing in popularity and as such it can be harder to get a place in the 'desirable' schools. You may find a waiting list or that you have to have interviews and exams at the same time as everyone else to have a chance of getting a place. No more just rolling up in the middle of the school year and getting a space.

School System In Mexico

School is mandatory between 3 and 15 but is available until 18. While even kindergarten completion is required by law, in reality, if a primary school will accept your child without them having completed kindergarten, SEP (the national education body) will allow it.

Maternal babies

Kinder 3-6 years old

Primaria 6 - 12 years old - Certificado de Educación Primaria

Secundaria 12 - 14 - Certificación de Educación Secundaria

Prepatoria 15 - 18 years old - Bachillerato

Most schools follow the curriculum laid out by the Secretaria de Educacion Publica. This is generally referred to as SEP. Some private schools are outside of the SEP programme and some use it as a base for their own curriculum.

Many kids will have gone to kindergartens that teach reading, writing, and maths, and will already have mastered the basics when they arrive in Primaría even if it isn't expected or required by SEP.

In a SEP school, grades are given out of 10. SEP requires a 6 to consider a year passed but many private schools will require a 7 at least.

Generally the school year begins in late August/early September and ends late June.

Many schools require you to provide both personal and class stationary and other bits and pieces required to run the school. Some schools just charge a flat fee and buy in bulk but others require parents to do the shopping. If you're coming from North America this may be considered normal, but for those of us from Europe this can be a shock. Now, on my third year of buying these items, I feel pretty confident about it but to begin with it was really hard.

TOP TIP: If you're buying stationary and don't know what something on the school list is, google it and click 'images'. This will show you exactly what it is you're looking for.

While the school year starts in Aug/Sept, the age determiner is 31 Dec. You cannot start primaria before the age of six but many parents opt to keep their children in kinder an extra year if they are young or have come from abroad and need more time to adapt. It is perfectly normal and accepted in Mexico and if it is something you're considering, it's absolutely worth discussing with prospective schools.

By the way, Madison is the only school offering a fully English language IB programme in Mérida in 2020.

School Paperwork: Mexico loves paperwork so yes, you will most likely be required to provide copies of birth certificates, CURP numbers[1], transcript records (our son, having completed only the last two terms of kinder in Mexico was required to provide not only a transcript from kinder but also a formal transcript from his school in the UK when we applied for his primary school). Some schools will allow you in without a CURP number, especially if you're in the process of getting residency.

Fees: Obviously the fees vary depending on the school and the age of the child. Schools charge an annual inscription (enrollment) fee as well as monthly fees (these can be paid monthly, termly or annually). Books and uniform costs extra and there are often requirements to contribute towards social events too. Rough costs for my children's school in 2020 are as follows (my kids are at a mid-level, mid-costing private primary school):

Annual Costs Per Child

Inscription (enrollment): $10,000 pesos

Technology costs (family): $500 pesos

Insurance: $500 pesos

Event costs (family): $600 pesos

Monthly fees: $5,000 pesos

Plus uniform, school trips, books, stationery requirements, teachers' day and birthday presents, and food.

Homeschooling is perfectly acceptable in Mérida and there is a good-sized homeschool community. You'll find plenty of information by searching on Facebook.

Honores a la Bandera: Many schools opt to have an allegiance to the flag ceremony. Some schools choose to do this once a week, generally on Mondays, and others once a month. Some won't do it at all. When I've seen it happen, a group of children have been chosen to parade with the flag while the other children stand with their arm held over their chests with the palm parallel to the ground. There is a pledge of allegiance and often songs such as "La Bandera de Tres Colores" (also known as the flag song) or the National Anthem are sung. A teacher may, or may not, give a speech.

My kids, as non-nationistic Brits, tend to suffer through this ceremony in silence although both can sing a great rendition of the flag song. We have told them we never expect them to pledge allegiance to any country including Britain or Mexico, but they absolutely must respect other people doing so.

School Hours: Generally school starts between 7 am and 8.30 am depending on the school and ends between 1 pm and 2.30 pm.

Schools that follow SEP take the first Friday of the month for teacher training so children are off school. This is called a día de consejo. There is no half-term break (as we have every term in the UK) but there are numerous official holidays and some months it can feel as if the kids are barely at school at all! We find that although school provides an official list of days off at the beginning of the year, *and* reminds us via the weekly bulletin *and* a note on the wall at the school gate, many parents, (ahem, us included) regularly get taken by surprise.

You'll find useful school focussed vocabulary in the appendix.

TWELVE

How To Buy A Car

O nly residents can buy cars legally. If you aren't a resident you'll either need to rent a car or find someone willing to buy on your behalf. With temporary residency you can bring your car from overseas for the length of your temporary residency permit. If you have permanent residency you need to formally import your car if you wish to bring it with you.

If you change your visa from temporary to permanent you'll either need to export and leave the car outside of Mexico or export and then officially import it back to Mexico. You can't legally sell a foreign car to another foreign resident without removing it from Mexico first.

Visitors need a TIP: Temporary Vehicle Importation Permit via Banjercito. A TIP is valid for 180 days.

If you're trying to figure out how to buy a car in Mérida, you may well be tearing your hair out as you realise this isn't a particularly fun or straightforward experience. We have bought two cars in Mérida now and have learned a lot about the process and the potential pitfalls during the time we've lived here. I have a full article outlining exactly what has to be done on mexicocassie.com. It can also be found in the appendices.

Our first attempt at buying a car was a depressing slog through the online *mercados*. My husband made so many calls and visited numerous overpriced cars that looked like they had seen better days.The people we called bothered to reply maybe 20% of the time, people responded to messages about 30% of the time, and our hit rate for seeing a car that reflected its true value was 0%, sadly, including the first one we bought.

It's embarrassing to admit that we were so tired of the process that when we saw a car that looked great on the outside we jumped at the chance to end this demoralising undertaking once and for all. We completely ditched all we knew about due diligence and bought an actual lemon. Fast forward two years, one costly breakdown (while on a trip to deepest Campeche) and over a dozen expensive repairs later, we needed a reliable (and more fuel-efficient) car. Dreading a repetition of the process, we jumped at the chance to use someone whose job it was to look for viable cars.

Top Tip: Use a service AND a trusted mechanic if you aren't buying a brand new car.

There are plenty of people who have created a niche for themselves helping foreigners and locals to buy roadworthy cars. We were initially against the idea of using someone to help us with something that should have been a simple process but in the end we gave in and now understand that it was the right thing to do.

Documents Required To Buy A Car In Mérida

Please don't buy a car that doesn't come with the original invoice. Just saying - sigh- yup, you guessed it, we know plenty of people who have made this mistake.

The owner of car must provide

- tax identity (*la tarjeta de circulación*) with a future expiry date
- photocopy of the seller's ID card (*credencial para votar*)

- the original invoice (*factura original*) from the car dealer

The buyer of car must provide

- cash, obviously
- photocopy of the buyer's ID card (*credencial para votar* or *tarjeta de residente*)
- proof of address (*comprobante de domicilio*)

Of course, the process of registering the car isn't simple or fun. You can either pay your finder to do most of it for you or you can struggle through on your own. The process is outlined on the Mexico Cassie website and the same detail is given in the appendices to this book.

Driving In Mérida

You should, as a resident in Mexico, get a local driving licence. In Mérida this requires you to pass a theory test that consists of ten questions, of which you have to get eight right. There is no official crib sheet, you just have to hope you know the answers.

Top Tip: If you speak Spanish, opt to take the test in Spanish as I've heard the English translation is not good at all.

You then take a practical test that consists of parallel parking your car between a set of cones. It sounds silly but people do fail. I loathe parallel parking FYI. Apparently it's possible to pay a company to teach you exactly how to parallel park to pass the test and then loan you their car to ensure you can't fail.

Mérida isn't a big city but there are a lot of cars on the road and traffic is getting worse year on year (in my opinion). I do drive here and I'm so used to it now that I worry about returning to the UK and being expected to follow all the rules to the letter.

- Roundabouts in Mérida are my particular hatred. Instead

of slowing down and using them as an opportunity to assist traffic flow, it feels to many foreigners as if locals use roundabouts as a chance to show how brave they are. It seems (I hope it isn't really true) as if many people choose to speed up as they approach the roundabout, assuming this guarantees them right of way.

- My husband loathes the roundabouts at the entrance to Progreso as they have different right-of-way rules to normal roundabouts. Watch the lines on the road to figure out what you're meant to do here.
- Indicating/using a turn signal is also not as important here as it is elsewhere. My kids find it hilarious that I will quite often tell them I love someone or I made a new best friend when I see a car indicating before turning.
- Lanes meander all over the place. Road markings are advisory. Follow traffic rather than painted lines when you're not sure. Be aware that roads such as Technologico pretty much require a 'dance' to navigate buses, cars turning, bikes stopping, and potholes. Do what you can, pay attention, and don't drive too fast.
- Much of Mérida is one-way, particularly in centro. Be warned though, that every now and again a road will become two-way for a block or two. You have to pay attention to road signs to know what's going on.
- Most crossroads have clear ALTO signs to let you know when you have the right of way. That said, always slow down at a crossroad, do not assume that all cars will stop because sometimes ALTO signs are missing or hard to spot. And of course, mistakes do happen.
- Topes, pronounced top-ez, (speed bumps) are a preferred method of controlling traffic speed. Watch out for them. Often they're signposted, but not always. Often they're painted, but not always. They are varying sizes and many will rock your car nastily when you miss them, which you will.

What to do if you get in an accident: officially, the rule is that you do not leave the scene of an accident until the police and the insurance companies tell you you may go. In reality often people who do not have insurance will leave before this can happen.

My husband was involved in a three-car-shunt when a car drove into the car behind him, which pushed that car into ours. There was negligible damage to all three cars so the two Mexicans involved determined between them (and my husband) that the best thing to do in this situation was to just pretend it never happened.

Petrol/Gasoline: Scams are known to happen at gas stations. I would recommend using cash only to pay for gas as one easy scam is to overcharge a credit or debit card. A card can also be skimmed for fraud. In Mexico attendants fill your car for you. They should always show you that the numbers have returned to zero before starting. You can either ask for lleno (full tank) or tell them how much you are spending. Don't forget to tip the attendants.

Public Transport: Mérida has a comprehensive public transport system made up of buses and minivans that transport people around the city for very little. There are also taxis that can be hailed, Uber is popular here (but not permitted at the airport), as is Didi. Personally, I've never encountered problems with taxi drivers from any of the services but I know others who have. Some women have reported sexual harassment from taxi drivers and they recommend always sitting in the back of a taxi for this reason.

Police Checkpoints: There are police checkpoints at the entrances to the state and the city. Yucatán is very proud of its reputation for being a safe state and takes this very seriously. Most of the time you just slow down and drive through as the police wave you on. If they want to check anything with you they'll wave you over to the side of the road.

There are often police checkpoints on the roads between the coast and Mérida as drink-driving can be a problem. On weekends and during vacation times, everyone is breathalysed as they leave the beach area.

THIRTEEN

Medical And Dental Care

I t took us a while to feel comfortable because the system is pretty different from the UK, but if you have insurance then the medical system is great. We have opted for a high excess on our insurance because for us, basic appointments at $600 pesos are affordable. As yet, we have been lucky enough not to require much more than that in the way of medical interventions. We have one kid who went through a phase of getting croup badly enough we had to take him to hospital a few times. We had to pay $600 pesos for the appointment plus whatever the drugs and syringes cost.

Hospitals in Mexico are classed as being either first, second or third level hospitals. There is, in 2020, only one official third (top) level hospital: Hospital Faro del Mayab, a new hospital that opened in 2019. These levels don't actually refer to the quality of service but to the range of services provided, despite what many assume.

If you don't want to pay out of pocket whilst in Mexico, either get private insurance, or as a permanent resident sign up for IMSS (Mexican government medical insurance). The 'best' hospitals don't necessarily take IMSS patients though and public hospitals can be crowded and require long wait times.

There are a number of hospitals in Mérida. My family uses Clinica de Mérida and Faro.

Clinica de Mérida was recommended to us when we first moved here. We've used the services many times for our kids when they've damaged themselves, got sick, or infected themselves with nasty bacteria as kids are wont to do. When I got the flu over New Year I went there, got a test and was in and out with a diagnosis and medicine within two hours.

Hospital Faro del Mayab, in the north of the city, just by La Isla shopping mall bills itself as the best hospital in South East Mexico. It's certainly beautiful and has a great reputation thus far. It is part of the Médica Sur network within Mexico, the only hospital chain to have an alliance with the Mayo Clinic in the USA.

Children's Medical Care: Unlike the UK, here in Mexico everyone has their own paediatrician. In Mérida it's perfectly possible to find someone who speaks English if this is a concern. Generally you'll then have the Whatsapp number of your doctor and you can ask questions as needed or call in an emergency. Obviously, call the office to make an appointment, don't ask the doctor directly.

Some of the pharmacies in Mexico also have doctors attached. If you think you know what's wrong or what you need, or you don't want to see a specialist, these pharmacy doctors are very useful. Some have a small fee to see the doctor and others are free but you're absolutely expected to tip for the service. Farmacias Guadalajara and Farmacias Similares tend to have the doctors attached.

TOP TIP: If you do use a pharmacy doctor, don't just automatically buy everything on the prescription they give you. Read it first because I guarantee they'll have added vitamins or Tylenol or other things you may not need. That's how this service pays for itself.

There are also psychologists, psychiatrists, speech therapists, nutritionists, physiotherapists and alternative therapists, and all the other medical '-ists' who speak English in Mérida. If you require specific testing for kids in English or specific speech therapy support you'll probably be able find it here.

FOURTEEN

Safety Talk Time

I give in. I really didn't want to write this section but I give in. I'll talk about safety. As I said right at the beginning, Mérida is considered to be the safest city in Mexico and that's why people from all over the country are flocking here.

So, what does safety look like in Mérida? Well, of course, we have crime. Nowhere is crime free. I don't leave my doors unlocked when I go out, I don't leave my car unlocked on the street, and I don't leave my purse or phone unattended anywhere. **That's just life in the twenty-first century.** That said, we do, at times, accidentally not lock doors; I do know people who have left their cars unlocked all night (you know who you are!) and while I don't leave my phone unattended on a restaurant table, it is regularly in my back pocket when I wander around town. In Mexico City, my husband's bag was stolen from under our noses in a café (damn, we let our guard down) because we had our 'Mérida level of vigilance on'. I don't feel as if that's likely to happen here but I guess it could do.

You will hear reports of violent crime against locals and newcomers in Mérida. It would be foolish to pretend everything is perfect here but I absolutely don't feel unsafe. I think my risk of being attacked or robbed in Mérida is lower than in the UK or USA. I feel safe walking around during the day and at night. Never once have I felt nervous or threatened. When we first arrived and I was a silly young thing, I'd walk around late at night having been out for many drinks with friends. I'm less likely to go out drinking these days (sigh) but that's more about age and work commitments than any change in my appreciation of safety.

People choose to live in privadas here for the space, not so much the safety. Many houses that aren't in privadas are behind walls or railings and many houses have bars on windows. That demonstrates clearly that there is not 'no risk at all'. However, good surveillance, the obvious presence of a fairly decently paid police force, and high arrest rates keep the city in order.

FIFTEEN

Real Talk. Finances. How Have We Made It Work?

I won't lie, obviously if there is a financial requirement for getting residency in Mexico, you have to be able to meet it to move here if you aren't lucky enough to have ties to Mexico. The figure can change depending on leadership. I have also heard that different embassies require different amounts. If you have regular online work, that will be accepted; if you have enough money in the bank that will be accepted. The embassy staff at your nearest embassy will help you figure out the best way to present your finances.

This is obviously a difficult chapter to write and I state here and now that yes, we are incredibly lucky and privileged that we were in a position where we could move country just because we felt like it. We aren't blind to that fact. We are lucky that we have always had good jobs that paid us enough that we could make small savings. Above I talked about how my job really was covering nursery fees but the truth is that my parents were helping out too. Without their help at some point, my job wouldn't have even paid enough to cover the fees for two small kids in nursery in central London. And we're the lucky ones because we have always had good jobs and parents who could help. That's so depressing for all of us, right?

Isn't that crazy? With all our privilege we still were only able to cover fees with help from my parents. We did have money that we were able to save before we had children. Again, we know that makes us very lucky. We used those to fund the first six month trip to Mexico. When we got back to the UK, Col got a job and I didn't. It didn't seem worth it given that we knew we were leaving again. I often required security clearance to work, which can take a while to get, and the school holidays would have eaten up my salary anyway when we'd have needed summer camps or child care. So I didn't work, but our daughter's nursery fees were finally subsidised by the state (from the age of three each child gets 15 hours free a week in the UK) and our son was finally in a state-run school so we were able to save a little.

Truthfully, because neither of us had ever worked remotely before, we were taking a huge risk by quitting life in the UK so my parents helped us by giving us a loan while we took this risk.

There. I said it. That's the truth. We couldn't have moved here without their help because we needed time to find jobs and a way to support our family. It took time. It took almost two years for my husband to find a decent online job and that wasn't easy for us. We're both hard workers. We hate taking money from other people and we absolutely worked our butts off to find a way to make money and make our life overseas viable.

In the UK I worked in the third sector in programmes management roles. Col is an IT guy. His skills were more obviously transferrable but finding opportunities for his specific skill set where he didn't need to be a US citizen wasn't easy. I have reinvented myself, professionally speaking. I have a blog, MexicoCassie.com, where I write about travelling around Mexico. I also write for travel magazines and I make my money editing magazines, articles, and novels, and offering online consultancy for people looking to move to Mexico. It hasn't been easy and we did need a bit of help to make it happen, but I'm very proud of us for managing all we have.

The cost of living obviously varies depending on how you choose to live. I guess we live a 'middle of the road' life in Mexico. We do have air-conditioning, we have two cars (mainly because one is a heap of junk), our kids are in private school, and we travel and eat well. However, we don't spend much on our house, our clothes, gadgets (I'm so mean, poor Col would love more gadgets) or 'stuff'.

Average Costs (in Mexican Pesos)

For this section I asked my husband to figure out our costs. He has been in charge of utilities since we moved to Mexico so I needed his head. He's currently sobbing in the bathroom now that he's actually looked at all our expenses as a whole. My suggestions on where to cut back were met with hollow laughter.

When looking at these, do remember that we live in a mid-range house, we don't use as much AC as others, but we do use it. Our kids are at a mid-range private school and we eat well. Food is probably the one area where we don't scrimp. We haven't included kid activities or vacation times in this breakdown, either.

Yearly costs

Rent: $180,000; $15,000 per month

Electric: $18,000; $1500 per month (bills: $800 - $4600 per 2 months)

Gas: $12,000; $3000 every four months

Food: $104,000; $2000 per week

Water: $1,800; $150 per month

Rubbish: $330; (includes $30 discount for paying for the year)

Internet: $6840; $570 per month

Cars: $60,000; $12,000+$30,000+$12,000+$6000 petrol+repairs+insurance+tax

School: $120,000; $5000 per kid per month + enrollment+misc expenses

Health Insurance: $30,000; two adults two kids

Total: $468,170 pesos

SIXTEEN

Negatives To Living In Mérida

O oooh, a hard question. Are there negatives to living in
Mérida? Well, nowhere is perfect, obviously. But I absolutely
don't, for one second, ever regret leaving the UK for Mexico.

Climate: For many, this is a negative. Mérida is famously hot. Six
months of the year are nigh on perfect and the other six months,
well, people call Mérida "El Inferno" for a reason. October to April
is pretty much perfect, a few weeks of needing sweaters and jeans
followed by perfection. Then the hot and hot/wet seasons come and
everyone has a mini meltdown. It's not just that temperatures can
reach over 40C, it's that these hot days are also often humid as all
hell. Sweating is absolutely the norm here. I regularly find myself
taking three showers a day.

You can't get in conversation with anyone, local or newcomer,
without a long weather discussion. I know this isn't just because I'm
English, because I see locals having this conversation on repeat and
it is pretty much the first thing people say, long before they know
where I'm from and make huge assumptions about my desire to talk
about the weather.

Living through the heat is different to travelling to somewhere hot. You're unlikely to have a house without air conditioning or a pool. If you don't have a pool you'll probably end up buying a small kid pool and using it to sit in. We don't go out much in the middle of the day, we alter our day to fit the weather. When it isn't global pandemic time, people use cafes, malls and cinemas to get their aircon fix. We walk in the shade, go out later, and eat a lot of ice-cream.

The rains tend to be a few hours most days in May, June, and July. It's generally heavy, tropical rain, tons of fun to watch if you're safe and dry, not fun if your house leaks or if you're outside. A heavy downpour is called an aguacero. It can last for a few minutes or a few hours. When you first arrive in Mérida you may laugh at the randomly different height pavements (sidewalks) and wonder why they're that way. Then you'll experience your first aguacero, see the centre of town flood in various places, and nod your head as comprehension dawns. They're high exactly where they need to be high.

Technically we are on the hurricane path so there are warnings every year and we are meant to be prepared but in reality, hurricanes are rare. We do get big storms every now and again. The norte winds over Progreso impact our weather and tend to bring some relief from the heat but we do also get the odd tropical storm. Actually I write this in the aftermath of Tropical Storm Cristobal, which wreaked havoc on Yucatán. We had something like 75% of our annual rainfall in three days. It is recommended to keep emergency rations of water, tinned food, batteries and candles for these situations.

Other negatives? Well, hmmmm.

Bureaucracy: bureaucracy is different and frustrating but I think every country's bureaucracy is differently frustrating. Here things sometimes seem to be unnecessarily complicated but I'm not sure I've ever found a country that doesn't feel that way.

Distance From Everything: for me, I sometimes feel that Mérida is far from the rest of the country because I'm from London and am used to just hitting up an airport whenever I want and flying direct to wherever I want. Mérida doesn't often allow that.

Green spaces: Mérida is a beautiful city and there are green spaces but they can be hard to find. The lack of easy access to park and great spaces to run and play is probably my least favourite thing about Mérida. I've written extensively on my blog about how to find places of natural beauty or places for kids to run and play.

Bugs: whoops, almost forgot about the insects. We just don't have many in the UK. Houses tend to not be immune to cockroaches, scorpions, various spiders, ants, or weird centipede things. You can fumigate professionally (I never have), spray with chemicals yourself, or try natural remedies (such as peppermint for ants), or you can accept life as it is in the tropics and invite them all in. We keep our kitchen pretty clean and try not to ever leave food out but even the tiniest crumb invites the ants in and if another insect dies in a corner of the room, ants arrive to eat it.

People living on the edge of town are more likely to be visited by little beasts than those in town. We've never seen a snake or tarantula in our house, for example, but friends living a little further out absolutely have. We get the odd opossum visitor in our garden, which is fun. I trod on a scorpion the other day, which was less fun. I definitely don't recommend doing that as it hurts.

For the ants, the best thing to do is to keep all food in boxes. Our pantry is full of large plastic boxes. Rice, flour, sugar etc is in its own packet, in a plastic bag and in a box. We occasionally get ants in the cupboard but rarely. They're too busy eating crumbs and honey spills left by the kids in the kitchen I guess.

I couldn't talk about bugs and not mention mosquitos. Honestly, they can be ferocious in Mérida. In our first house I had to sleep with repellant on as they were so bad. It really depends on where you live and the time of year. For a week or so after tropical storm

Cristobal in 2020, for example, we were inundated with large mosquitos that were apparently brought inland by the winds.

If you live near standing water you'll probably have more mosquitos to deal with, that's one reason why people can be wary of living next to empty lots. The city does spray when mosquitos are at their worst, but you'll probably want to keep repellant on hand.

SEVENTEEN

Final Thoughts

I think that's all I have for you, for now. Obviously, I'll keep on writing more as we explore more of Mexico and have more and more experiences worth sharing. You'll be able to find these exciting stories on my blog, mexicocassie.com.

Not for one second do we regret leaving our home country to begin again in Mérida. My kids feel at home here and so do we. We will continue learning and growing and deepening our roots in Mexico. Even 2020 and all it has thrown at the world hasn't made us want to go back to the UK. We adore our life in Mexico, the friends we've made, the opportunities for life that exist here, and we don't miss the UK very often at all.

But that's my family's experience.

Life in Mérida, like anywhere, is what you make of it. Come with an open mind, accept that Mexico won't function in exactly the same way as the place you left behind and that's ok. It might feel weird to begin with, you might want to complain, to judge and compare, but seriously, try not to do that as it won't help you settle in. I don't mean you shouldn't acknowledge that moving country can be hard, because it absolutely can be hard, scary and exhausting, but it's also wonderful, exciting, and opens so many doors. You can acknowledge how hard things are without becoming one of those people who sit and whine about their new home!

Try everything, meet everyone, be open to new experiences, and you'll have a great time.

And you know what, if it doesn't work out for you, that's ok too. It's ok to try a new place and find it isn't what you expected or hoped for and go home or find somewhere else.

Of course, you should absolutely be using mexicocassie.com to keep on learning about Mexico and life here and if you want even more from me, why not use my consultancy service and book an hour of one-to-one time with me where you can ask me anything (within reason).

Good luck with your adventures in Mexico!

Notes

11. How To Choose A School

1. CURP stands for Clave Único de Registro de Población - basically a unique ID number for residents and citizens of Mexico.

Where To Find Mexico Cassie

Blog: mexicocassie.com

Facebook: facebook.com/mexicocassie

Instagram: instagram.com/mexicocassie

Acknowledgements

This book would obviously never have happened if we hadn't moved to Mexico. I'm so very grateful to my family, particularly Col, for always being up for adventures and for never complaining (too much) when I drag everyone off to check out somewhere or something new and for supporting me when I said I wanted to start a blog about our adventures in Mexico.

Monique, while you haven't chosen to come on adventures with us (weird), you're absolutely integral to the creation of this book. Your unending support and belief in me pushed me to do this. Thank you.

And Las for bullying me into writing this book, I owe you one!

Appendices

House Vocabulary

Provisional Sale Agreement - Convenio de Compra/Venta

Official appraisal of the Land - Avaluo

Annual property tax - Predial (pay on January 1st or soon after)

Bathroom - Baño

Bedroom - Recamera

Bill - Cuenta

Contract - Contrato

Deposit - Deposito

Damp - Humeda

Endorsement - Aval (you often need this to rent. If you don't have one then you'll pay additional deposit)

Ejido - Community owned land

Estate agent - Agente Imobiliario

Fideicomiso - Trust

For rent - Renta

For sale - Venta

Garden - Jardin

Gated community - Privada

Kitchen - Cocina

Landlord/landlady - Casero/dueño/propietario or casera/dueña /propietaria

Lawyer - Abogado

Living room - Salón

Modernised - Modernizada

Monthly - Menusal

Mortgage - Hipoteca

Notary - Notario

Offer - Oferta

Pool - Piscina/alberca

Renovated - Renovada

Rent - Renta

Roof - Techo

Room - Habitacion

Town house - Town house

Vendor - Vendedor

School Vocabulary

Classroom - Aula / salon

Coordinator - Coordinador

Folder - Carpeta

Grades (as in results) - Notas/ calificaciones

Head teacher - Principal

Holidays/Vacation - Vacaciones

High school - Secundaría (lower) and Prepa (final years)

Homework - Tarea

Lunch - Lonch (because school lunch is more of a snack than actual lunch)

Meeting - Cita / junta / charla

Notebook - Cuaderno

Nursery - Kindergarten

Playground - Patio

Primary - Primaría

Private school - Escuela particular/privada

Recess - Recreo

Report - Boleta de calificaciones

Teacher - Maestra /maestro

Public holidays

Jan 1st - New Year's Day

Feb Día de la Constitución - officially the 5th, but the celebration is the first Monday of the month

March 16th - Benito Jaurez birthday

April 30th - Día de Niño (taken seriously in Mexico)

May 1st - Labour Day

Mother's Day (not a national holiday but an important day)

September 16th - Independence Day

October 12th - Día de la Raza (Columbus Day)

November 2nd - Hanal Pixán (Día de Muertos)

16th - Revolution Day

December 12th - Día de la Virgen de Guadalupe

25th - Christmas Day

Easter dates (Easter, Good Friday and Maundy Thursday - obviously are moveable feasts)

Useful Phone Numbers

General emergency: 911

Ambulance: 925 2056 (although personally I'd ring Faro or Clinica de Mérida direct)

Red Cross Ambulance: 969 935 1624

Police: 969 935 0026

Fire Service: 116

Green Angels (free roadside assistance): 078

CFE: 071

JAPAY: 999 930 3450

Zeta Gas: 999 941 0100

Abimerhi: 999 240 1571

Eight Steps To Getting Your Temporary Residency: FULL ARTICLE

This vital yet dull post is brought to you by my wonderful husband, Colin. He has been in charge of our Mexican residency applications the whole way through. It has been left to him for two simple reasons:

1. We decided that we would apply for his temporary residency in Mexico first and the rest of us would apply later as his dependents. In order to do this, I had to set aside all my feminist leanings (I lean hard, by the way) and accept this was the best option since it was the cheapest option and we all know cheap is best, or at least, it was in this case.
2. bureaucracy is super dull and I didn't want to do it.

Please note that this article is written based solely on our experiences. We take no responsibility for any changes to the system or problems you encounter! We aren't Mexican immigration officials, just residents wanting to share our experience in the hope of easing the lives of others.

Say a word multiple times and it should lose its power. The word I'm specifically referring to is "bureaucracy" and it still makes me feel a bit queasy even though I've said it **a lot** recently. From my experience so far, on the bureaucracy scale of 'super efficient and necessary to circumlocution office', the needle of Mexican bureaucracy points just right of centre. It feels like a prize to have finally been awarded my temporary resident visa for Mexico in 2018 (and three-year resident visas in 2019).

Mexico has made things very simple for tourists. For visits up to six months you can go anywhere in Mexico and don't need to hassle yourself with anything more than completing an FMM (Forma Migratoria Múltiple) on the plane, a guilty smile at immigration (elicited by all officials in circumstances such as these) and '*ya*' (that's it). Because tourist visas are so simple to acquire, it was pretty tempting for us to just top up a tourist visa every six months but then we decided we wanted to do things properly. Not only is there a constant worry of an official crackdown on people doing this but there is also a very real sense of wanting to do things by the book – fair play and all that. (Other) Brits complain about illegal immigration all the time so it just felt that we couldn't just waltz into another country illegally.

After speaking with the Mexican consulate in London, with the funds we had, they advised the following. One person, who can prove a cash float of around £62,115.00 (amounts seem to vary country to country), should apply in London for a one year temporary residency visa and the rest of the family can apply in Mexico for a one year visa as dependants. The visa process, therefore, is started outside of Mexico for the person with funds (entering Mexico with a special visa) and the family members enter as tourists and apply to change status whilst in Mexico.

Of course, many choose to use the services of a lawyer or relocation company to finalise their residency status in Mexico. We decided to do it ourselves. Why? Good question. Maybe because it's cheaper but maybe a little bit because we were convinced we didn't need to be beaten by the system, especially the system in a country we want to live in. If we want to live here then we have to be able to navigate it, right?

Right.

Step 1 to Acquiring Temporary Residency in Mexico

1. Create account and make an appointment with home country consulate. Make sure you give yourself enough time to collect all your paperwork outlined in this step. The

relevant web page is: https://mexitel.sre.gob.mx/citas.
webportal/pages/public/login/login.jsf

2. Download, print, and complete a visa migration form. At the web page: https://www.gob.mx/tramites go to: Migración, visa y pasaporte -> Visa para extranjeros viajando a México -> Visa de residente temporal. You can click on the top right phrase "**Descargar Formato**" (download form).

3. Don't forget you have to list, in writing, the documents you are providing on the visa application form.

4. Print out proof of required cash float for the previous year. Since the consulate wants to see a year's worth of financial statements amounting to over £60k this meant pulling together a number of different accounts for the entire year. Given that each bank statement can be over three pages each month, this can be a lot of paper to take with you to your consulate appointment. I used a mixture of the following to cut down the amount of paper I needed:

5. I tried an online mechanism to download a whole year (in a format as official looking as possible).

6. A screenshot of a whole year (or as few screenshots as possible)

7. Four separate monthly statements at equal intervals throughout the year, or screenshots of same.

8. Note: When any of the documents only showed an account number, and not my name or address, I asked the bank to send me a page stating my name, address and the account numbers together. This was either by the bank's secure messaging, email (if you're lucky), or snail mail for the older style banks. It goes without saying that if you have other income, print out proof of the other sources, for example, a rental agreement.

9. On the day of the appointment bring the following:

10. Passport, original and photocopy of photo page

11. Visa application form

12. Payment in cash

13. Photocopies of proof of income documents

You may well assume you'll be going to the consulate for a formal interview but actually, it felt more like an informal chat. It felt like it helped that the woman interviewing me remembered Cassie from an earlier discussion, but who knows?

You'll need to return to the consulate to collect your passport a couple of days later. If you are successful then you get a Mexican visa page in your passport giving you 30 days from the time of entry to start the process to swap (*canje*) the visa for a year's residency. Also, you are given six months to enter Mexico and start the process. We found out later that once accepted by the consulate in London, everything following is mere formality, you've already been approved for residency.

(Cassie adds that while it may be a formality that clearly doesn't mean you can make ANY errors at all in your dealings with INM)

This is the only part of the process where an office keeps your passport for any length of time. In Mexico, they will look at it, but never keep it.

Step 2 To Acquiring Temporary Residency In Mexico

Go to Mexico. You need to fill in the FMM (Forma Migratoria Múltiple) on the plane as normal, BUT SHOW IMMIGRATION THE VISA PAGE so they don't stamp your passport with a tourist visa. If they do, the process has failed right here.

Step 3 To Acquiring Temporary Residency In Mexico

1. Fill in web form: http://www.inm.gob.mx/index.php/ page/Solicitud_de_Estancia.
2. Choose "Canjear documento" and "Canje de FMM por tarjeta" options from the drop down menus. Fill it in and

print out, this form will be needed later and it's useful to show it so you can obtain the correct additional forms.

3. Go to your local INM (Instituto Nacional de Migración) office and collect the following additional forms that aren't available on the internet.

4. Formato Básico

5. Carta de Solicitud de Canje. For the "Carta de Solicitud", there are two important points to note for this form: under "activities in Mexico" write "*Viviré en México de mis recursos provenientes de mi país*" (I will live on funds earned in my home country whilst in Mexico). Do not try and be clever. Do not write anything else.

6. *Aviso de tratamiento de los datos personales y notificación electrónica*

The FMM number required is the one underneath the barcode on your original entry form. They may give you a sheet of instructions too. Of course, it would be helpful if these were all downloadable, instead of having to wait at the INM office, but you are going to need to practice your patience and this is a good place to start. Just go to the desk and ask for "*los formatos para canjear documento migratorio*" and show them your web form.

In Mérida the INM office is open between 9:00 until 13:00. I generally arrived at 8:30, and tended to have fewer than ten people ahead of me, making a relatively painless waiting experience but arriving after 9am or later leaves you wide open to misery and frustration!

The process normally goes like this: (a) sign-in and guard gives you a number; (b) number is called and they give you forms or, if the forms have been filled in, a window number; (c) go to window and they check the forms and process you (until they find an error and then you're out on your ear until you fix it).

Step 4 To Acquiring Temporary Mexican Residency

1. Go to INM office early because you have to go to the bank in-between processing. Bring the following:
2. Money (approx MXN $4000 for 1 year temporary residency)
3. Passport and a photocopy of both the photo page and Mexican visa page
4. The web form you printed in the previous step
5. The three filled-in forms collected in the previous step (check carefully for errors as none are permitted)
6. I was then given a bank form and sent to pay for my residency. Any bank will do. Ensure you get a receipt.
7. Go back to the office. This time, instead of queuing, I went straight to the desk to ask if I could go back to the same window to complete my processing and they let me.

Once I had completed the process I received:

1. A piece of paper with NUT ID (Numero Único de Tramite) with web address to view application status and about an hour after I left the INM office – https://www.inm.gob.mx/tramites/publico/seguimiento-tramite.html
2. An email with my password to access the online system so I could keep track of my status:

They also asked me to make an appointment for fingerprinting; there were no appointments available for six weeks so here, I had a hiatus.

Step 4 (mezzanine step) To Acquiring Your Temporary Mexican Resident Visa

Twelve days later I received an URGENT EMAIL asking me to hand in my 'Carta de Solicitud de Canje'. This turned out to be a renewal document (*renovación de documento migratorio*) asking for exactly the same information as the original '*Carta de Solicitud de Canje*'. If you get this form change, again, under "activities in Mexico" put "*Viviré en México de mis recursos provenientes de mi país*" and put the FMM number (under the barcode). I have a theory that the form had changed midway through my "*trámite*", but who knows, maybe they spilt coffee on my original.

Step 5 To Acquiring Temporary Mexican Residency

I received my "resolución" about 18 days after step 4. I logged in and under "notifications" downloaded the folio "*resolución*", which stated "success" and the start and end dates of my residency – the year starts from the date of arrival in Mexico. Since my fingerprint appointment was already booked it was just a matter of waiting. At the bottom of the web page was a place to fill-in more data, which I did, putting "home" as the most reasonable choice in a limiting drop-down menu under "activity in Mexico", plus other personal details (height, weight, etc) that I wrote on my Formato Básico.

Step 6 To Acquiring Temporary Mexican Residency

Get your photos taken at a place that knows about the requirements of INM. Photos must be on matte paper, size infantil (2.5 x 3 cm): 2 x front and 1 x right side – no white clothes, forehead and ears uncovered, no earrings, no glasses.

Step 7 To Acquiring Temporary Mexican Residency

I went to my fingerprint appointment with:

1. Passport
2. Photos
3. Appointment slip and form with my NUT ID
4. NOTE: appointment slip said bring "*Formato Básico*" but they had kept that form in step 4

When I arrived I was given a 'waiting' number as per usual but went straight to the desk and asked them if it was necessary. It wasn't, and they checked my appointment on the computer and called me to a window minutes later.

I received originals of the *"resolución"* documents from step 5 and a *"constancia"* (certificate) with my CURP (Clave Único de Registro de Población) identification number. I wrote *"recibí documento original"* and signed some documents for INM. Lastly, I did *"mis huellas"* (fingerprints) and was told to return in a week for my residency card.

Step 8 To Acquiring Temporary Mexican Residency

Collect card. Yey.

Family Reunification Process and Temporary Residency

This article covers the next step many of us need to go through whilst obtaining a family temporary resident visa for Mexico: that of completing the 'family reunification visa' process. This is the process you'll need to follow, if, like our family, you decided your best option was to obtain a temporary residency visa for one family member, let others enter on a normal tourist visa (FMM) and convert to temporary residency once in the country. This is often considered to be the most sensible option open to families wishing to move to Mexico. Indeed, it was recommended to us by the Mexican Embassy in London because it's the cheapest way of getting everyone here legally.

This is a process for obtaining residency for a spouse and children, via the person who has

already obtained residency.

Just to set expectations I will try not to mince words; this particular process can be laborious, frustrating and expensive.

Simple Errors To Avoid When Completing The 'Family Reunification Visa' Process in Mexico

Many people will tell you this is not something you should attempt to do alone, that you need to hire a lawyer or an agency to help you. You can, of course, do that but we don't think you *need* to. The process isn't cheap and while we paid with our time, we also saved a great deal of money by doing it ourselves, and we learned a lot about Mexico and its bureaucracy in the process.

Be prepared to be sent away by INM if your papers aren't 100% perfect.

We thought we were incredibly careful but we still made tiny errors and encountered problems we couldn't have foreseen. We hope this list of reasons we were sent away might help you have a smoother run than we did:

1) Official translations "*perito traducciones*" will probably always have errors in them – so check every word and number of that multi-page document. A single document like a birth certificate will turn into a seven-page "*perito traducción*": 1 for the certificate, 1 for the apostil, 4 pages for translating every corner of the aforementioned documents, and 1 page with the translator's photo and license. Every page must be stamped and signed.

2) One INM rule is they can never take original documents. This even applies to the "*perito traducciones*" which, even though contain photocopied certificates, once signed and stamped are promoted to "originals". INM will only accept photocopies of the 7-page documents for each translated certificate – so buy a big folder and don't show up without your photocopies of everything.

3) Don't just trust when the photo shop that says your photos are INM compliant. On the fingerprint appointment slip, it says *exactly* how the photo must be. Take this slip to your photo session and ensure the instructions are followed to the letter. Of the four of us, two had to redo our photos because we trusted the photo shop to know what they were doing

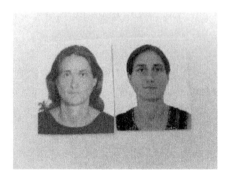

Photo on the left is not ok as you cannot see Mexico Cassie's ears. Hair down is fine as long as forehead and ears are completely visible.

4) When I filled out forms on the INM website, I didn't see that a bug in the website changed a field (a note about this later). INM noticed it of course and sent me away to fix it.

Now, without further ado, the process.

Step-By-Step Instructions To Obtaining Family Temporary Residency In Mexico

Obtaining Family Temporary Residency In Mexico: Step One

Go to this web page: https://www.gob.mx/tramites, then choose:

Migración, visa y pasaporte -> Condiciones y estancia en México -> Cambio a residente temporal por vinculo familiar.

Press the button to fill in the form.

Choose *"Cambiar condición de estancia"* and *"Cambiar condición a residente temporal por unidad familiar"* options from the drop-down menus. You should have the option of adding any kids to the same *"tramite"* (process). In this example of one spouse and two kids, you will end up with one *pieza ID* and three NUT IDs. Fill it in and print out all the forms, they will be needed later and it's useful to show them so you can obtain the correct additional forms.

NOTE: at the time of writing there was a bug on the website that kept changing the country of origin from "Reino Unido ..." back to México after "submit" but before "continue" – so before going to the next person – review the entries!

Go to your local INM (*Instituto Nacional de Migración*) office and collect these additional forms for each person. Ask for *"los formatos para cambio de condición a residente temporal por unidad familiar"* and show them your web forms.

- *Carta de Solicitud* – *cambio de condición a residente temporal por unidad familiar* (spouse and child forms are different)
- *Aviso de tratamiento de los datos personales y notificación electrónica*

- *Hoja de Ayuda el pago en ventanilla bancaria* (bank payslip for $1266 pesos with reference numbers on it)

Again, I can't stress how much going half an hour before opening time eases the pain. In Mérida, the INM office opens from 9:00 until 13:00.

Obtaining Family Temporary Residency In Mexico: Step Two

Go to a bank with your *"Hoja de Ayuda ..."* and pay $1266 pesos per person to start the "change of state" process. The slip is so that the bank can issue the appropriate electronic stamps, with correct names and reference numbers, for your process. Once you have the receipt with an electronic stamp you won't need the help slip anymore. Note that this fee is only for the "change of status via family member". The actual residency fee comes later. Eek.

Obtaining Family Temporary Residency In Mexico: Step Three

Collect all forms together in a big folder. You keep the originals but you may need to show them at INM.

- passports and residency card for the resident
- apostillised birth certificates and marriage certificate
- *perito traducciones*: birth certificates, marriage certificate
- (spouse's birth certificate was included too – see "name change" in step 4 below)

In Order to Convert The Spouse's Visa Into Temporary Visa You Need:

- FMM (*Forma Migratoria Múltiple*)
- INM web form (*Formato para solicitar tramite migratorio de estancia*)
- *Carte de Solicitud – Cambio de condición a residente temporal por unidad familiar*
- *Aviso de tratamiento de los datos personales y notificación electrónica*
- Photocopy of passport for spouse

- Photocopy of passport for resident
- Photocopy of residency card (back and front)
- Bank receipt with electronic stamp for $1266
- Photocopy of *perito traducción* of marriage certificate
- Photocopy of *perito traducción* of birth certificate (see "name change" in step 4 below)
- Extra photocopy of *perito traducción* of birth certificate of one child (see "name change" in step 4 below)

In Order To Convert A Child's Visa Into Temporary Visa You Need:

- FMM (*Forma Migratoria Múltiple*)
- INM web form (*Formato para solicitar tramite migratorio de estancia*)
- *Carte de Solicitud – Cambio de condición a residente temporal por unidad familiar*
- *Aviso de tratamiento de los datos personales y notificación electrónica*
- Photocopy of passport for child
- Photocopy of passport for resident
- Photocopy of residency card (back and front)
- Bank receipt with electronic stamp for $1266
- Photocopy of *perito traducción* of birth certificate

Notes on filling in the forms:

DO NOT BOTHER DEVIATING FROM THESE NOTES AS YOU WILL PROBABLY BE SENT AWAY OR BE TOLD TO REDO THE FORMS. THESE ARE THE RESPONSES INM WANTS TO SEE.

Carte de Solicitud (spouse):

- "*casado(a) con*" means "married to", so put the resident's name
- "*vinculo con*" means "[family] link to" so put "*certificado de matrimonio*" next to that

- next to *"actividades"* put *"vivir a lado y bajo la dependencia económica de mi esposo/a"*
- next to "western existential crisis" tick the box: "come to terms with being economic dependent of spouse"

Carte de Solicitud (kids):

- Next to *"poseo vinculo con _____ de nombre _____"* put *"mi padre"* or *"madre"* and resident's name
- Next to *"vinculo con el acta de"* put *"nacimiento"* (birth certificate)
- Next to *"actividad"* put *"vivir a lado y bajo la dependencia económica de mi padre/madre"*

When you sign any of the kids' forms:

- The resident signs with their full name and signature, plus the phrase *"en representación del menor"*
- The form *"Aviso de tratamiento de los datos personales"* put the resident's email and the above phrase, however, since there was no place for the child's name, put *"Hijo/a*: child's name" in brackets at the bottom

Obtaining Family Temporary Residency In Mexico: Step Four

Go to the INM office with all your paperwork and expect something to be amiss.

Our personal name change story:

Often in the UK women change their surname at marriage. MexicOCassie did not as she's a ranty old feminist and is no one's property, damn it. However, when we decided to have kids she felt she didn't want either of us to have a different surname to the kids. Long discussions ensued where we discussed new names – Sparkle or Ninja were her favourites, the possibility of blending names was discussed but eventually, we opted to take one of our surnames for the entire family. It was a democratic, feminist decision.

However, when moving to Mexico, this means that the person who changes their name ends up with what the Mexicans consider to be a discrepancy in their paperwork: the name on the passport is different to the name on the marriage and birth certificates. This is officially A Problem.

Here it is important to note that US and UK citizens with name change problems will find themselves in a different situation. US citizens require, according to our US friends, an affidavit from their embassy stating that the documents are all correct. In Mérida, this isn't so hard as there is a US Consulate in town.

As Brits we have no consulate here so when we were sent away to deal with this issue we got right on with trying to figure out the best way to solve it. This is what we did:

- We called the nearest consulate in Cancun. We found a number on the internet. The Canadians picked up and told us the number was no longer correct and we needed to phone the British Embassy in Mexico City
- We called our embassy in Mexico City. No one picked up at any point. We tried every single option the phone menu gave. No one picked up. We couldn't leave a message as the inboxes were full
- We panicked and emailed the Mexican Embassy in London. They were confused as they'd never heard of this issue
- We panicked
- We fumbled around on Facebook asking if anyone knew anything because there aren't actually that many Brits trying to get residency in Mexico at any one time.
- We eventually managed to make contact with a very helpful member of staff at the British Embassy who informed us that INM were wrong to demand this paperwork from us as there is a high-level agreement between the UK and Mexico stating that British women with name changes resulting from marriage do not require an affidavit from the embassy.

This immediately sounded far better than one of us having to fly to Mexico City for an embassy visit. This kind individual sent me a letter stating this clearly and advising INM in Mérida to talk to their colleagues in Mexico City

- We took this letter to the INM officials, but they rejected it because it didn't have an original signature and stamp. We tried to explain the following points:
- Requiring a UK citizen to supply an original "government level agreement" letter, signed and stamped, would defeat the purpose of the agreement. This is something that can be checked by immigration officials. (That didn't go down well).
- We brought proof; an extra copy of our child's birth certificate which has both surname and maiden name. Surely, this is better than an "oath"?
- We brought a birth certificate, with the same name as the marriage certificate. Surely, this too is better than an "oath"?
- After much consulting with other INM officials and at least two visits from us, they finally said, and I'm paraphrasing here: "Bueno, we can file your application, but if anything's amiss you need to resolve it within ten days, otherwise you forfeit the fee. Good day to you sir, and don't darken our doors again with your UK weirdness."

Obtaining Family Temporary Residency In Mexico: Step Five

Forms accepted(ish). Probable success. Tis done. Take a deep breath and relax.

Obtaining Family Temporary Residency In Mexico: Step Six

Ten days later we received an email asking us to log-in to review the status, which thankfully was successful. Here we had two jobs for each person after logging in (each person has a separate NUT ID):

- Resolution: download and print the resolution, which

includes another *"Hoja de ayuda el pago en ventanilla bancaria"*, ie. bank slip for paying the approx. $4000 pesos per person – gulp!

- Add personal details using the link labelled *"Para la expedición de su Forma Migratoria, registre o actualice sus datos aquí."* I entered education, height, weight, previous job, and current activity in Mexico ("home" from a dropdown menu seemed to be the most appropriate).

Obtaining Family Temporary Residency In Mexico: Step Seven

Go to the INM office and make an appointment for fingerprinting the whole family. You don't need to queue for this, just go and speak to the person on the front desk.

Obtaining Family Temporary Residency In Mexico: Step Eight

Go to a photo shop that knows the requirements of INM photos, but check them too just in case (see fingerprint appointment slip for details on photo requirements).

Obtaining Family Temporary Residency In Mexico: Step Nine

Go to a bank and pay the approx. $4000 pesos using the *"Hoja de ayuda … "* and get the receipt with electronic stamp.

Obtaining Family Temporary Residency In Mexico: Step Ten

Go to the fingerprinting appointment (with kids). The slip of paper tells you what you should have done and what to bring.

- you will have already filled in the *"Formato básico"* in step 7, so tick this one off
- passports
- bank receipt for payment
- photos
- kids

If you're us, get turned away because the photo shop didn't know how to take pictures that would satisfy immigration. Run to photo shop to get new photos taken and run back.

Finally, get certificate (*Constancia*) with CURP ID.

Obtaining Family Temporary Residency In Mexico: Step Eleven

You will have to log in over the next week to check for messages "payment received" and "documents ready for collection". Then simply, go and collect the cards (without kids).

Hurrah. If you're still alive then you've made it and your family is now officially the proud owner of residency cards for everyone! Time to celebrate and start counting down the days until you have to return for the annual renewal process!

How To Buy A Car In Mérida

If you're trying to figure out how to buy a car in Mérida, you may well be tearing your hair out as you realise this isn't a particularly fun or straightforward experience. We have bought two cars in Mérida now and have learned a lot about the process and the potential pitfalls during the two years we've lived here.

In this article my husband (who writes all the technical and bureaucratic articles because I'm super kind and tend to leave all the bureaucracy to him while I swan about 'researching' cool places to take trips in Mexico) explains exactly how to buy a car and is also super honest.

Our first attempt at buying a car was a depressing slog through the online *"mercados"*. I made so many calls and visited numerous overpriced cars which looked like they had seen better, no, they actually looked like they had never seen better days. The people I called generally picked up 20% of the time, people responded to my messages about 30% of the time, and my hit rate for seeing a car that reflected its true value was 0%, sadly, including the first one I bought.

I was tired of the process and when I saw a car that looked great on the outside I jumped at the chance to end this demoralising undertaking once and for all. The part of my brain that does meticulous due diligence was overridden. Its cry of *"this will be the start of bigger problems"* were ignored.

Fast forward two years, one costly breakdown (whilst on a trip to deepest Campeche) and over a dozen expensive repairs later, we needed a reliable (and more fuel-efficient) car. Dreading a repetition of the process, I jumped at the chance to use someone whose job it was to look for viable cars.

Top Tip #1 For Buying A Used Car In Mérida

Use a service. *There are plenty of people who have created a niche for themselves helping foreigners and locals to buy roadworthy cars. We were initially* *against the idea of using someone to help us with something that should have been a simple process and something that we were convinced we could do on our own.*

We chose Pol Gomez Bolivar. We found him on Facebook. He charges 5% of the cars' purchase price, and this includes the price of his mechanic checking the car and Pol's support with the paperwork. Pol speaks good English.

For us, the only service in which I was interested was the "finding a decent car" since we have (finally) a mechanic who we trust and we are now well versed in Mexican bureaucracy.

Once we liked a car that Pol found, our mechanic checked the on-board computer and identified some minor problems during a test drive. I wanted the problems fixed so we negotiated a reduction in price. Pol took $3000 MXN as a deposit and went to the seller to buy the car on our behalf.

Yes, you are paying extra for a middle-man but (a) if you are happy with the price and (b) if the result is a car that doesn't need a part replaced every three months then it will be money well spent.

Once Pol came back having put down the deposit for the car, he brought with him

- the car's tax identity with a future expiry date (*la tarjeta de circulación*)
- a photocopy of the owner's identification (*credencial para votar* or anything official with a CURP)
- the original invoice with the following on the back: the date, the words "*CEDO LOS DERECHOS DE ESTE FACTURA AL SR XXXX (*name in capitals as per your passport)" the owner's signature, and the owner's full name in capitals as per their
- identification

Documents Required To Buy A Car In Mérida

Owner Of Car Must Provide

- tax identity (*la tarjeta de circulación*) with a future expiry date
- photocopy of the seller's ID card (*credencial para votar*)
- the original invoice (*factura original*) from the car dealer with text as outlined above on the back

Buyer Of Car Must Provide

- cash
- photocopy of the buyer's ID card (*credencial para votar* or *tarjeta de residente*)

Top Tip #2 For Buying A Used Car In Mérida

I also, for completeness and my own peace of mind, chose to do the following

- took a photo of the middleman's ID card (*credencial para votar*)
- wrote a contract (*contrato de compraventa*), which the middle-man, buyer, and witness signed
- had a witness for the whole process

Steps For Completing The Purchase Of A Used Car In Mérida

If you don't feel the need to have someone walk you through the whole process, this is what you'll need to do (correct as of October 2019).

Before you start this process, be sure to have a hearty breakfast!

1. **Buy insurance**. You need insurance **before** you can change ownership of the car.

2. **Immigration Letter part 1** (new requirement). You need to head to the Police at *"Registro De Control Vehicular"*. This is located behind Costco. (Google maps will find this no problem. Confusingly,

I have noticed some Yucatán sites refer to "Secretaria de Seguridad Publica, Mérida" and "Centro de Servicios Yucatán, Mérida" in relation to registering car ownership. The names are plastered on different sides of the same building.)

From there, as a foreigner, you need to get a letter requesting that immigration (INM) give you a letter confirming your registered address, one that is identical to that on the proof of address you will provide later. The name can be different but the address itself must match. There is an information desk that will take your IDs into a small room and return with a letter from the police.

3. **Immigration Letter part 2.** To get this INM address letter, now you need to go to INM and take

- your passport and photocopy of relevant pages
- ID card and photocopy of relevant pages
- proof of address (eg. water bill) and photocopy (it doesn't matter if it has your landlord's name on it)
- letter from police

In the new INM building, there seems to be a special line for this process. I handed in all copies plus the police letter. The documents are checked, a high official signs your *constancia* and it is returned to you by another designated official. When this process works smoothly it can take a couple of hours. A mix of lengthy queues and availability of the designated officials conspired to make this process two days for me so be aware it may not go as fast as you expect. The *constancia* also had some errors in it, which were dealt with swiftly once pointed out.

IMPORTANT: make sure the name on the *constancia* is identical to your full name as per your passport and the address on the *constancia* is identical to the proof of address you are providing, including the *cruzamiento* (ie. the x y part) if it is written on your proof of address.

4. **Tax Number.** Changing ownership gives you a new tax identity for the car. This is also done at the *"Registro De Control Vehicular"*. Go

to where it says *"Centro de Servicios Yucatán"* and into the door on the side of the building marked *"Registro De Control Vehicular"*. This is where the fun starts. You will need:

- letter from INM
- proof of address (*comprobante de domicilio*) and photocopy of the front
- car invoice (*factura*) and double-sided photocopy
- photocopy of the previous owner's ID (*credencial para votar*)
- car tax identity (*tarjeta de circulación*)
- insurance (*seguro*) and photocopy of all sheets
- ID card (*tarjeta*) and photocopy
- passport and photocopy

The *Registro de Control Vehicular* opens at 8:00 am. I got there half an hour early and when the doors were about to open someone from the information desk came out to give us all numbers. They have a useful screen with those being processed, so it is easy to know when it's your turn.

Once you hand in all the documents, they check them and ask you to sign a document and a slip of paper. They return the slip and ask you to wait while they complete the process. Once your name is called, your originals (car invoice, insurance, and proof of address) are returned.

You can then go to the *"caja"* area and await your name to be called again so you can pay the fee to get your new car tax identity, your *tarjeta de circulación*, with the same expiry date as on the previous *tarjeta*. You will also receive a payment slip labelled *"tenencia"*.

NOTE: they did not ask for my rental agreement even though the water bill had the landlord's name on it. Neither did they ask me for my driving license.

Printed in Great Britain
by Amazon

84674467R00068